Sugar Skulls
Design & Coloring Book

This book belongs to

_____

Here's one to get you started and give you some inspiration.

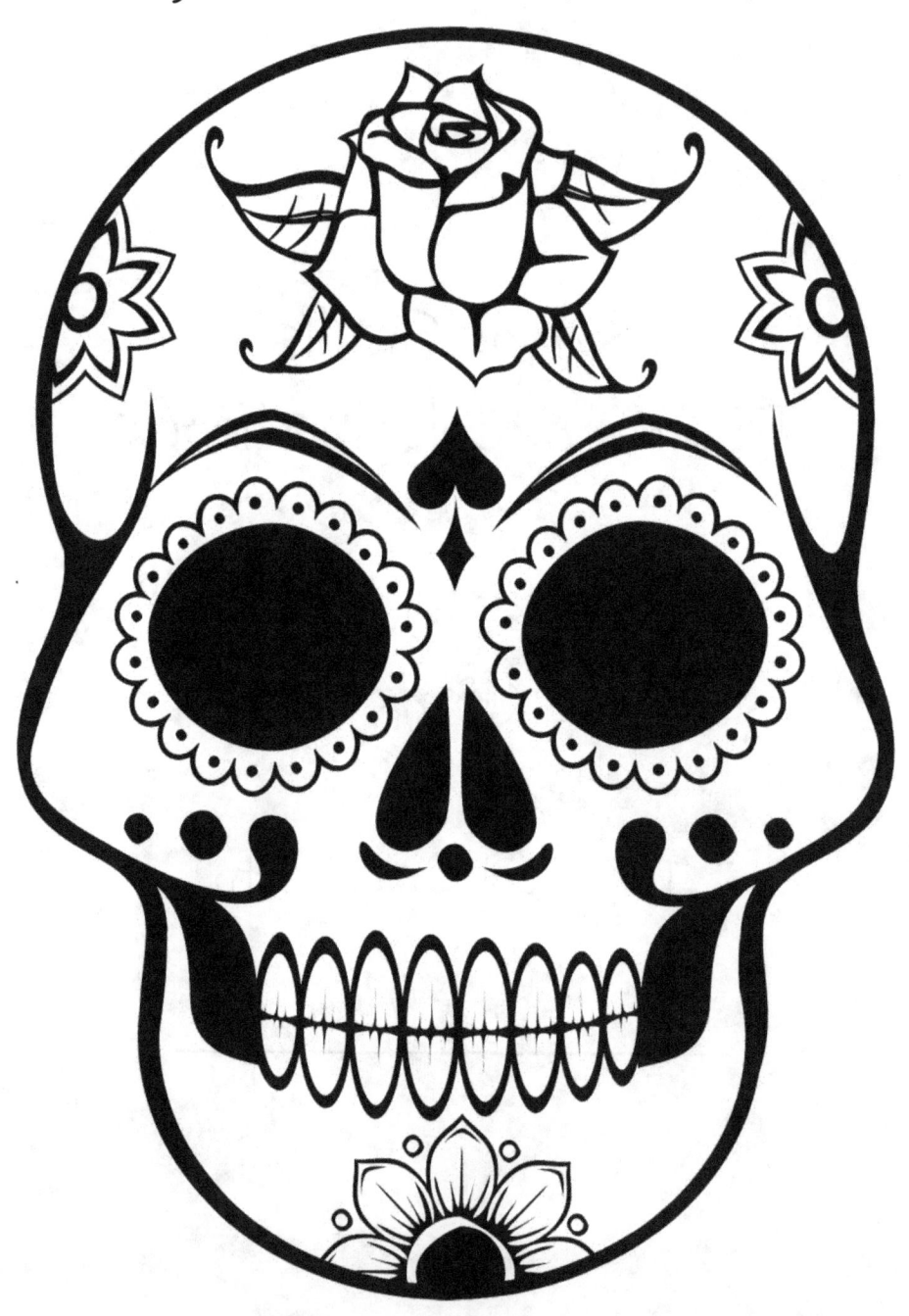

Now it's your turn...

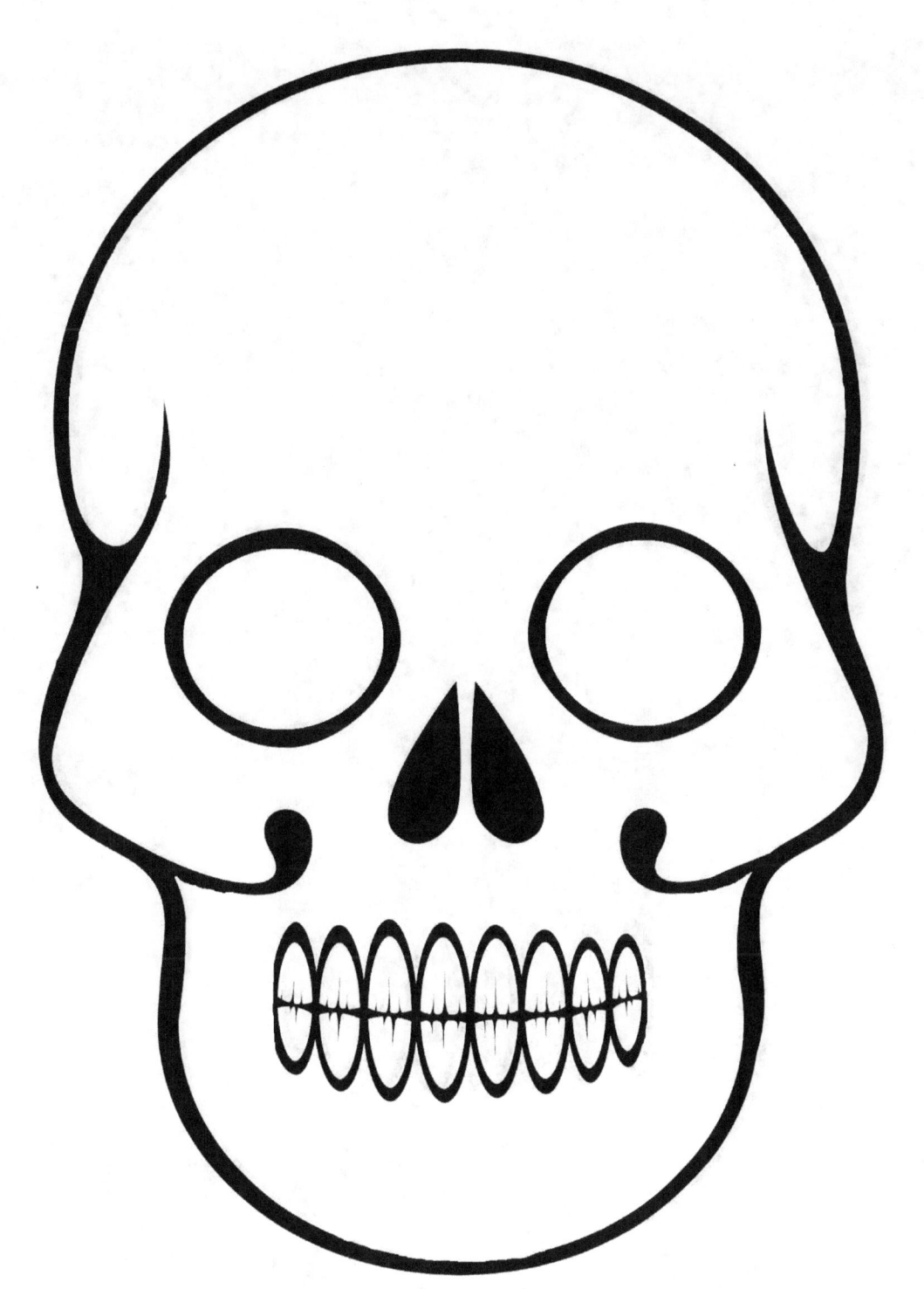

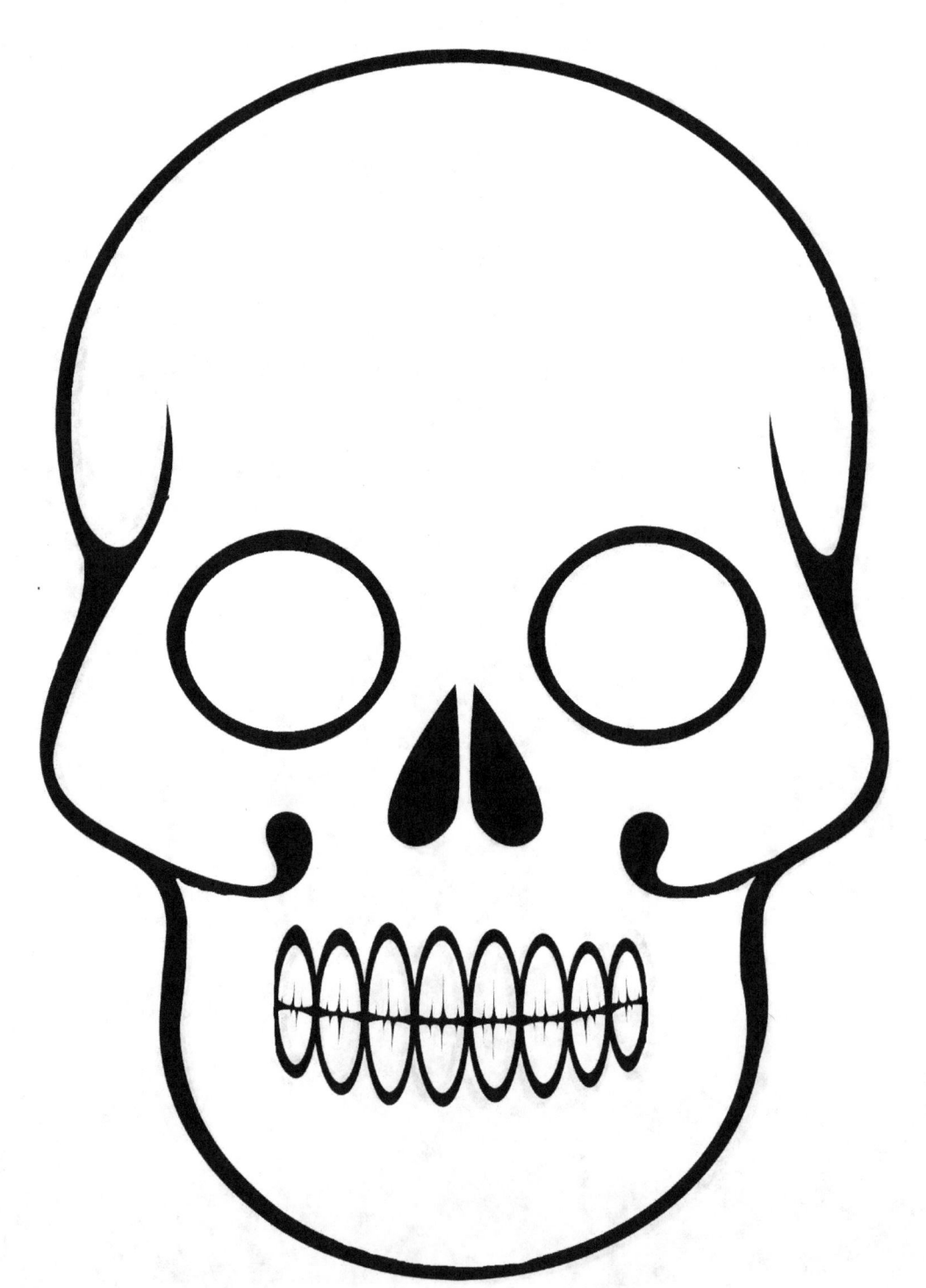

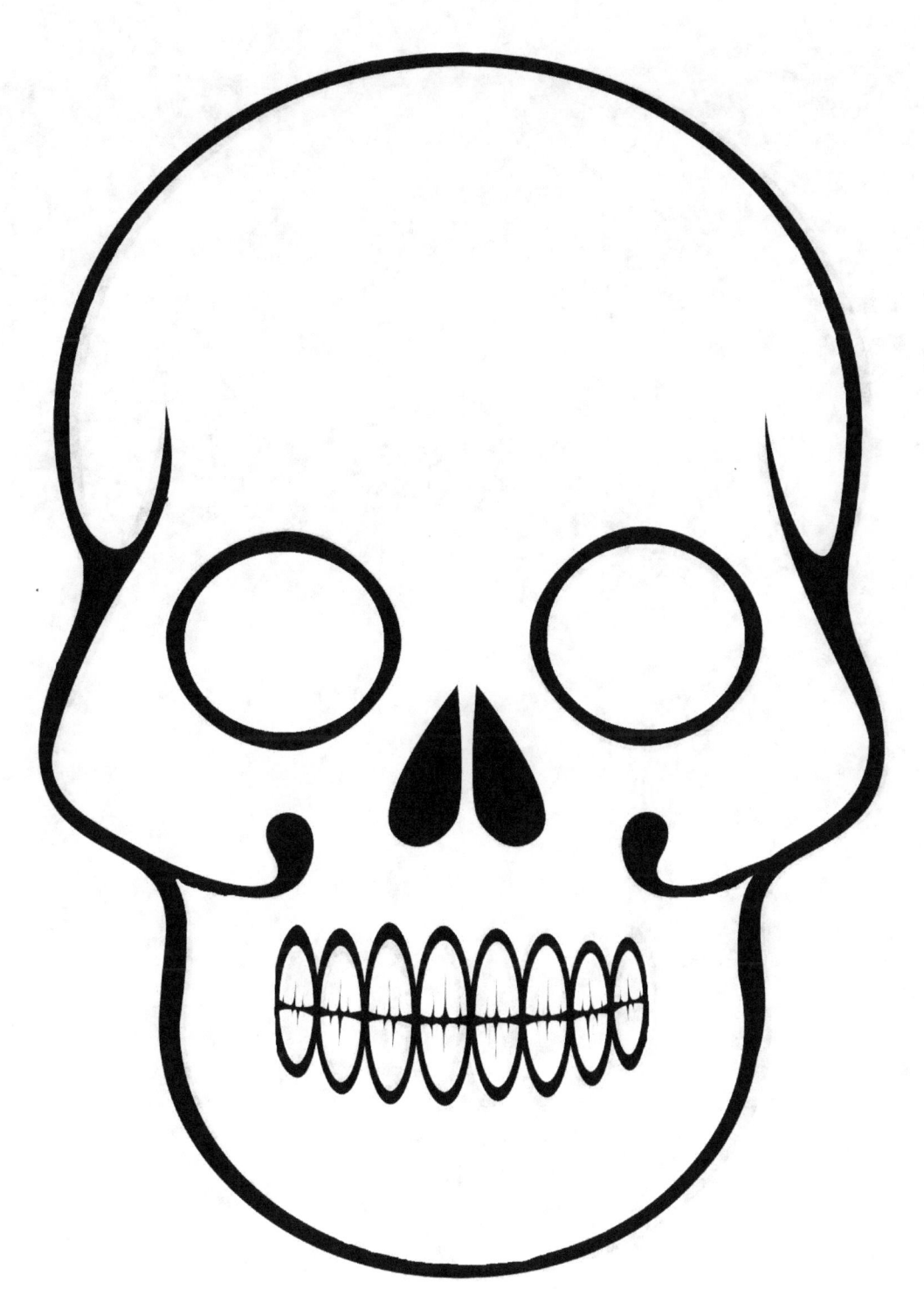

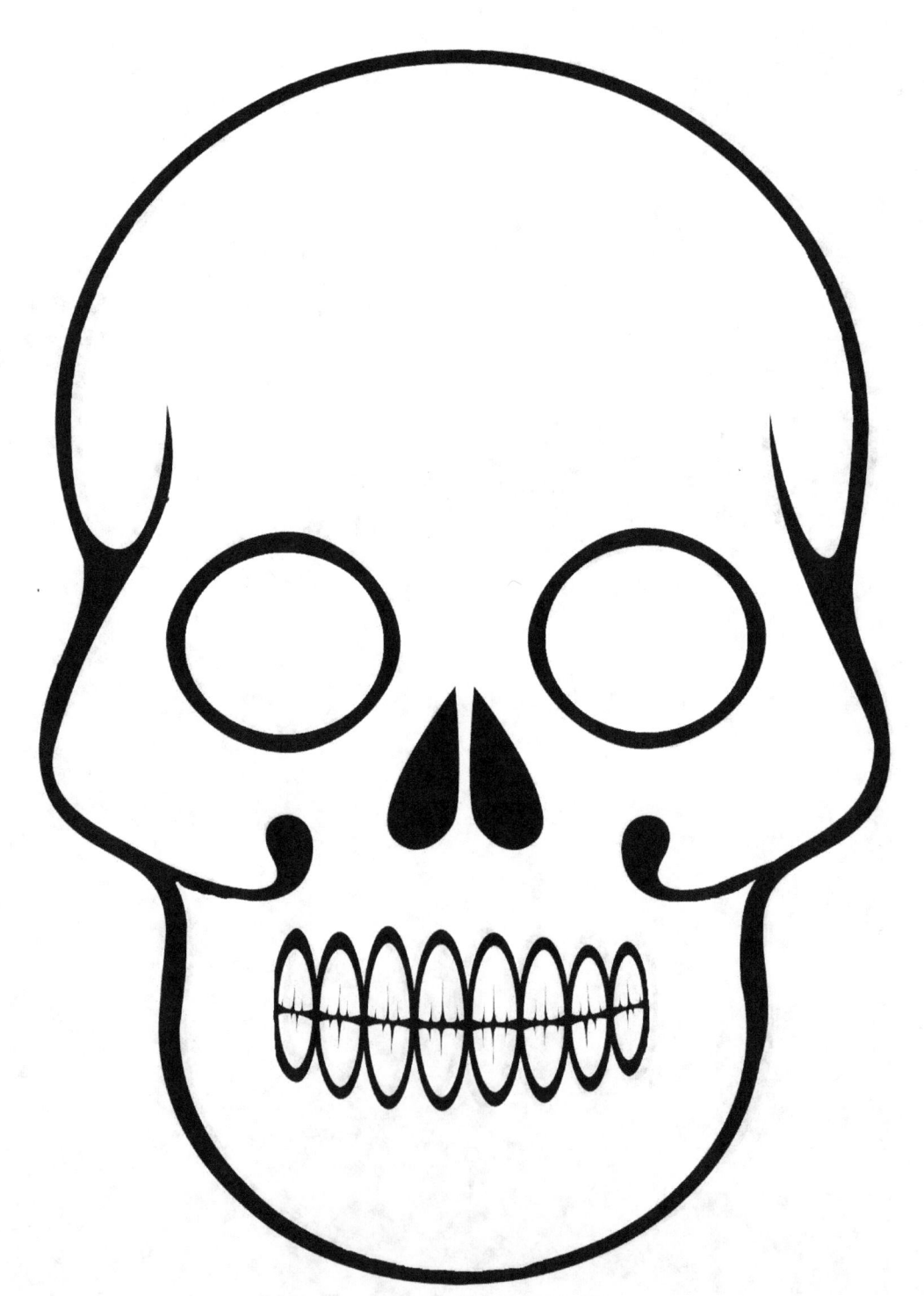

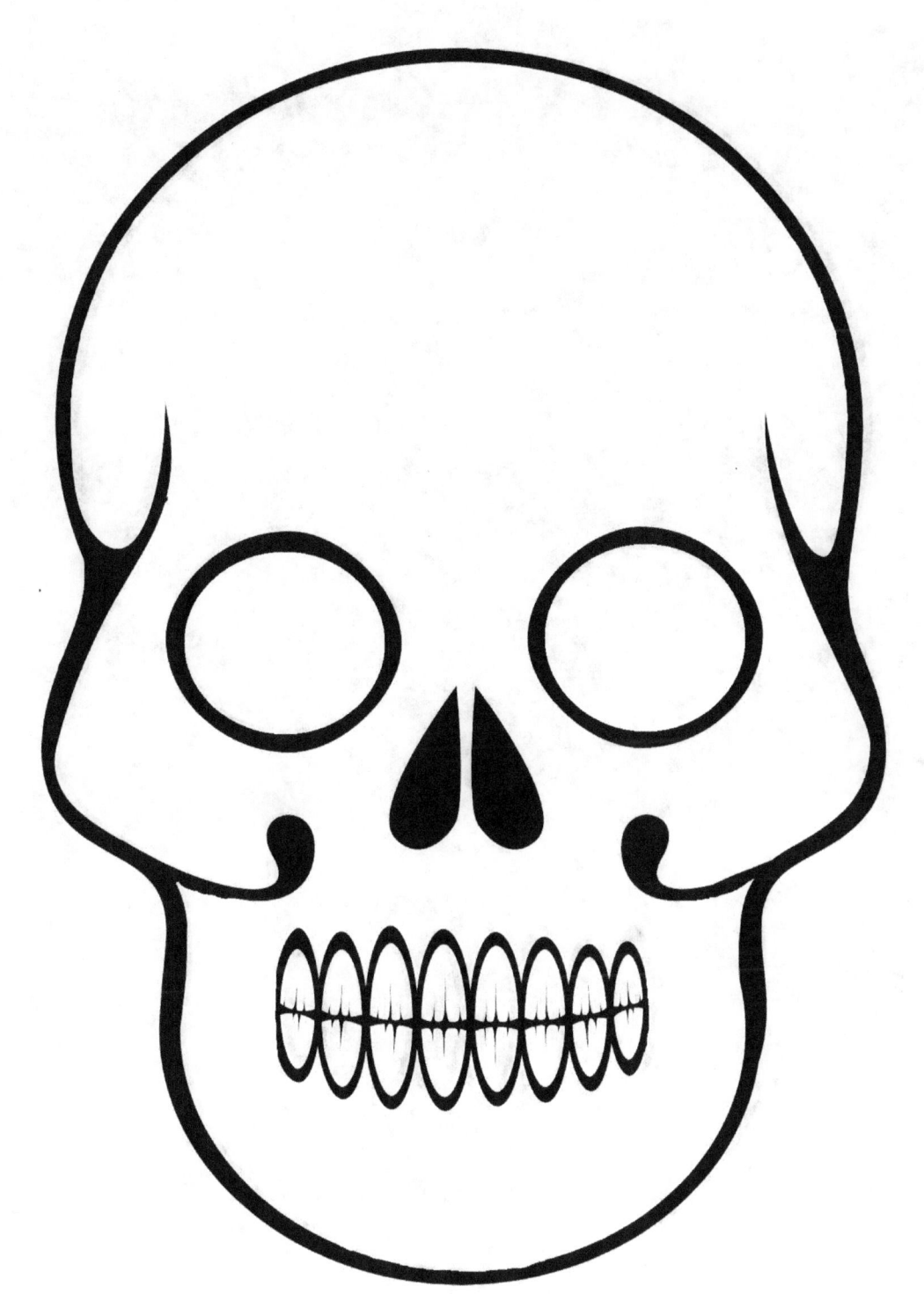

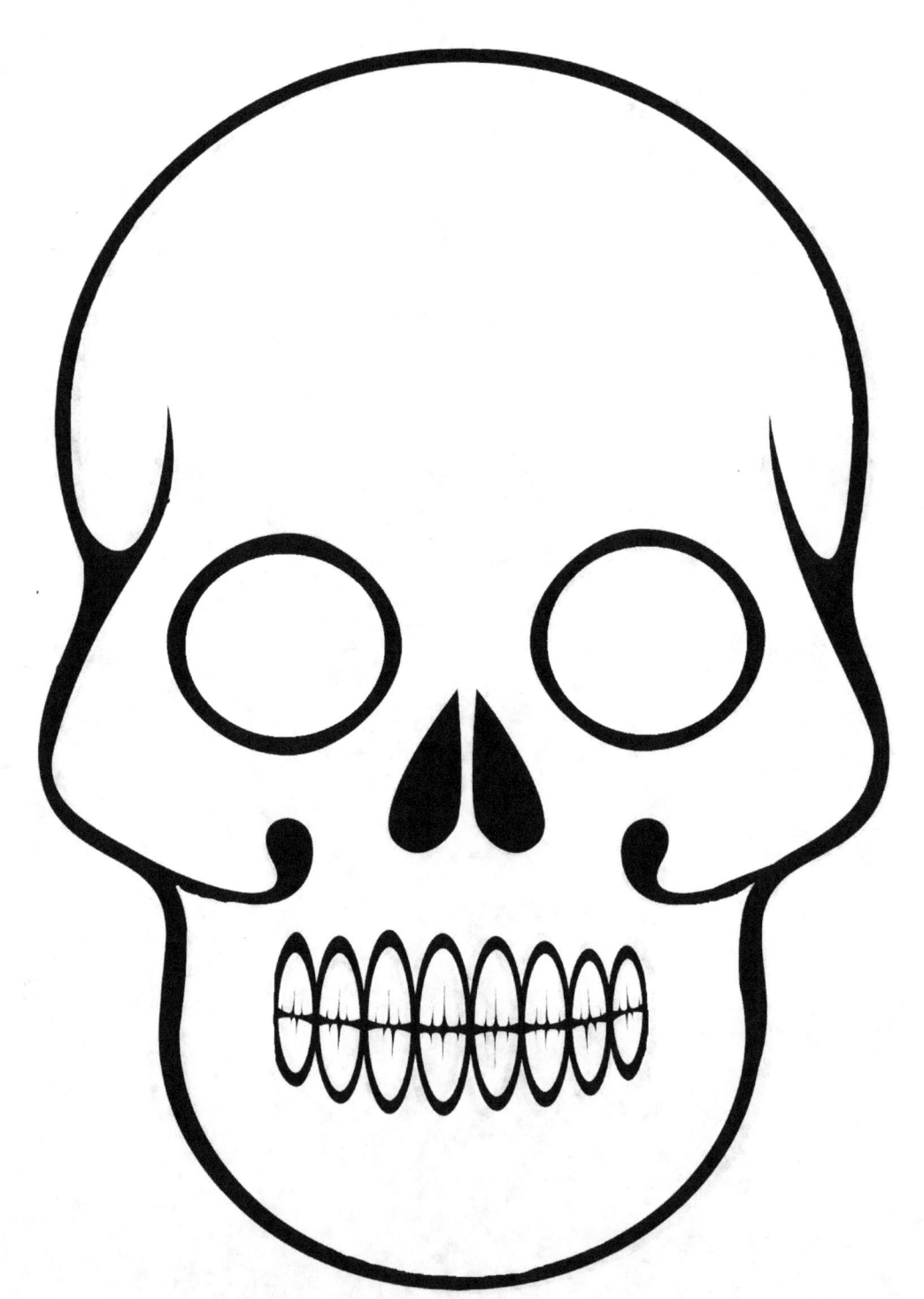

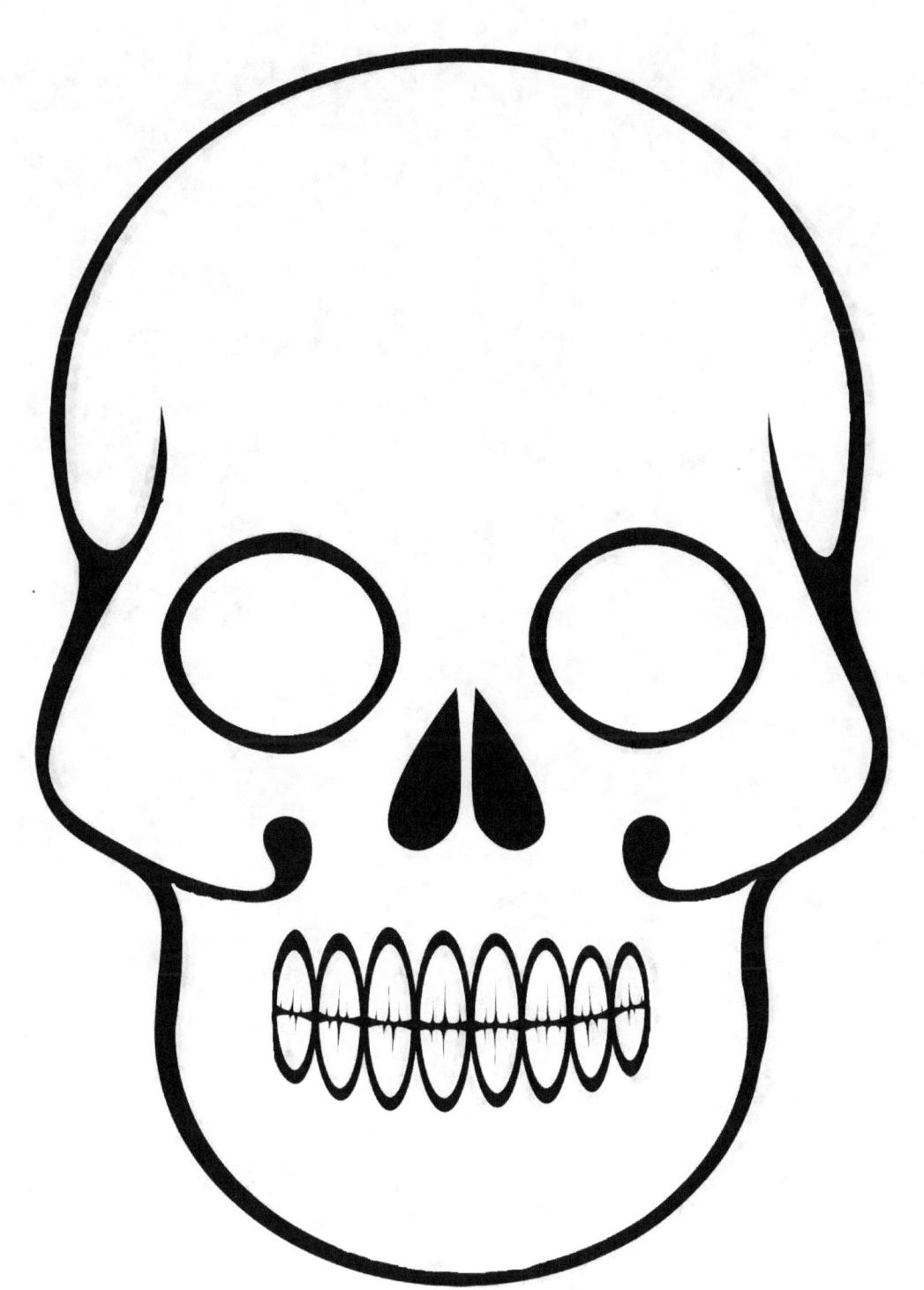

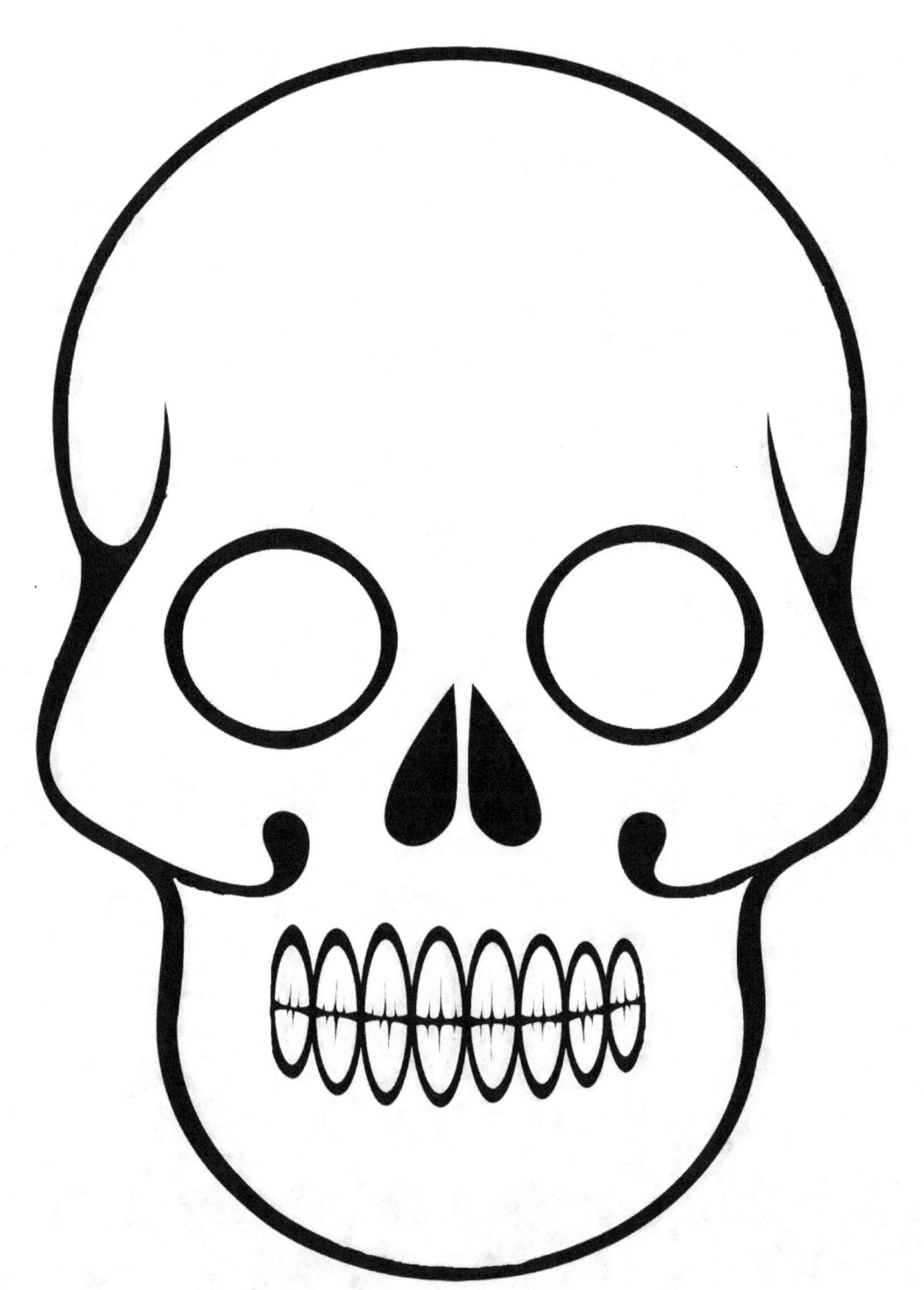

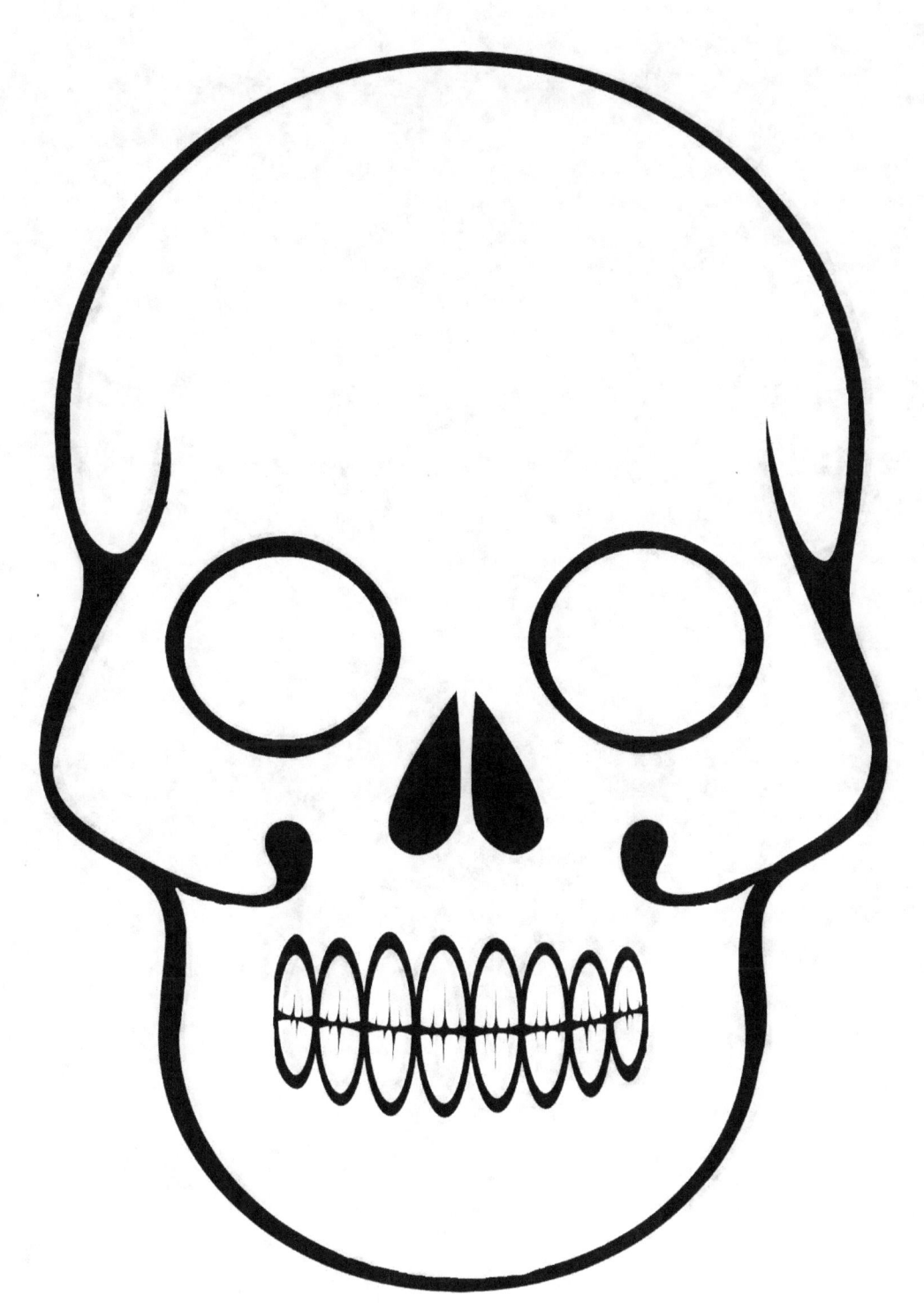

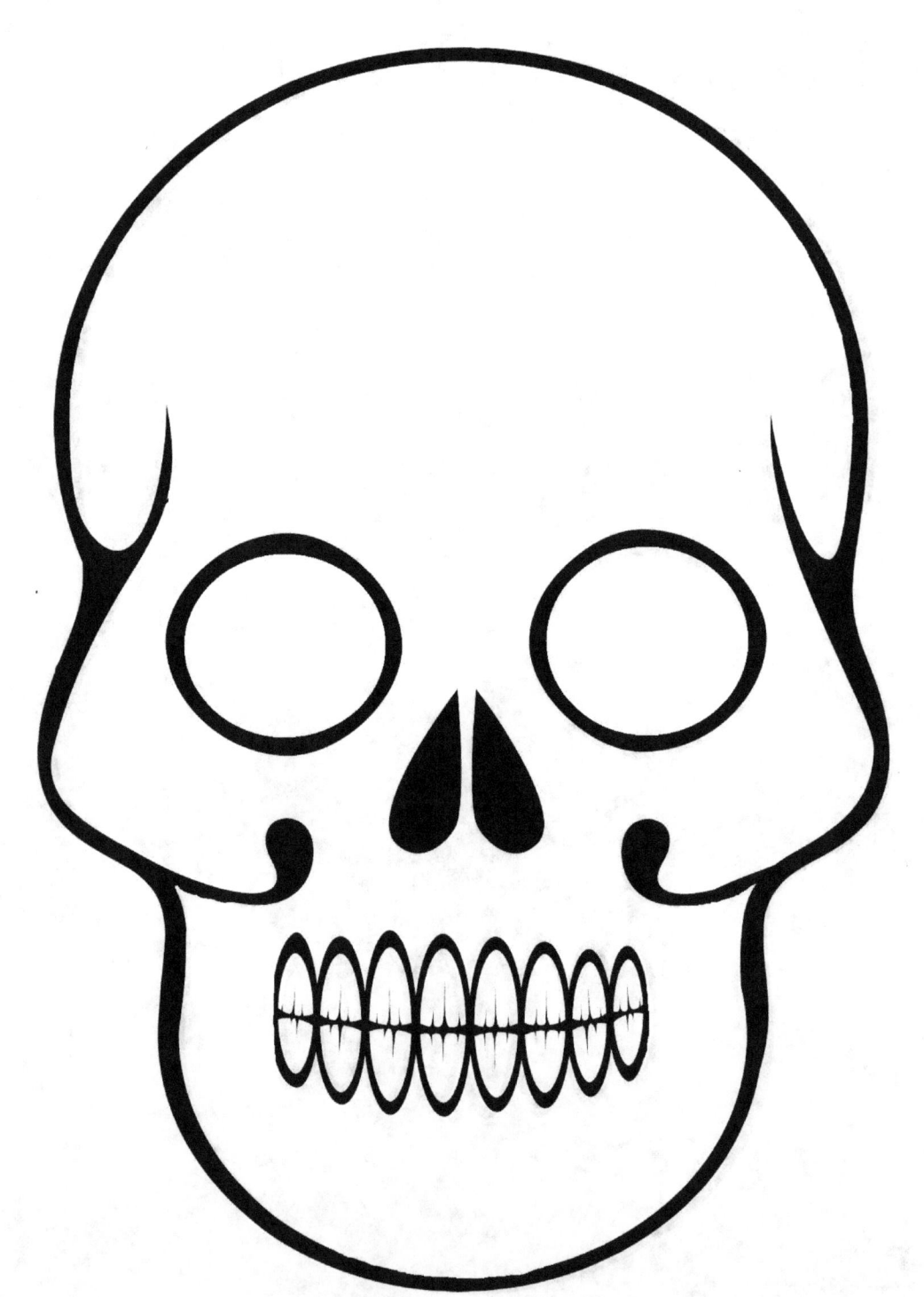

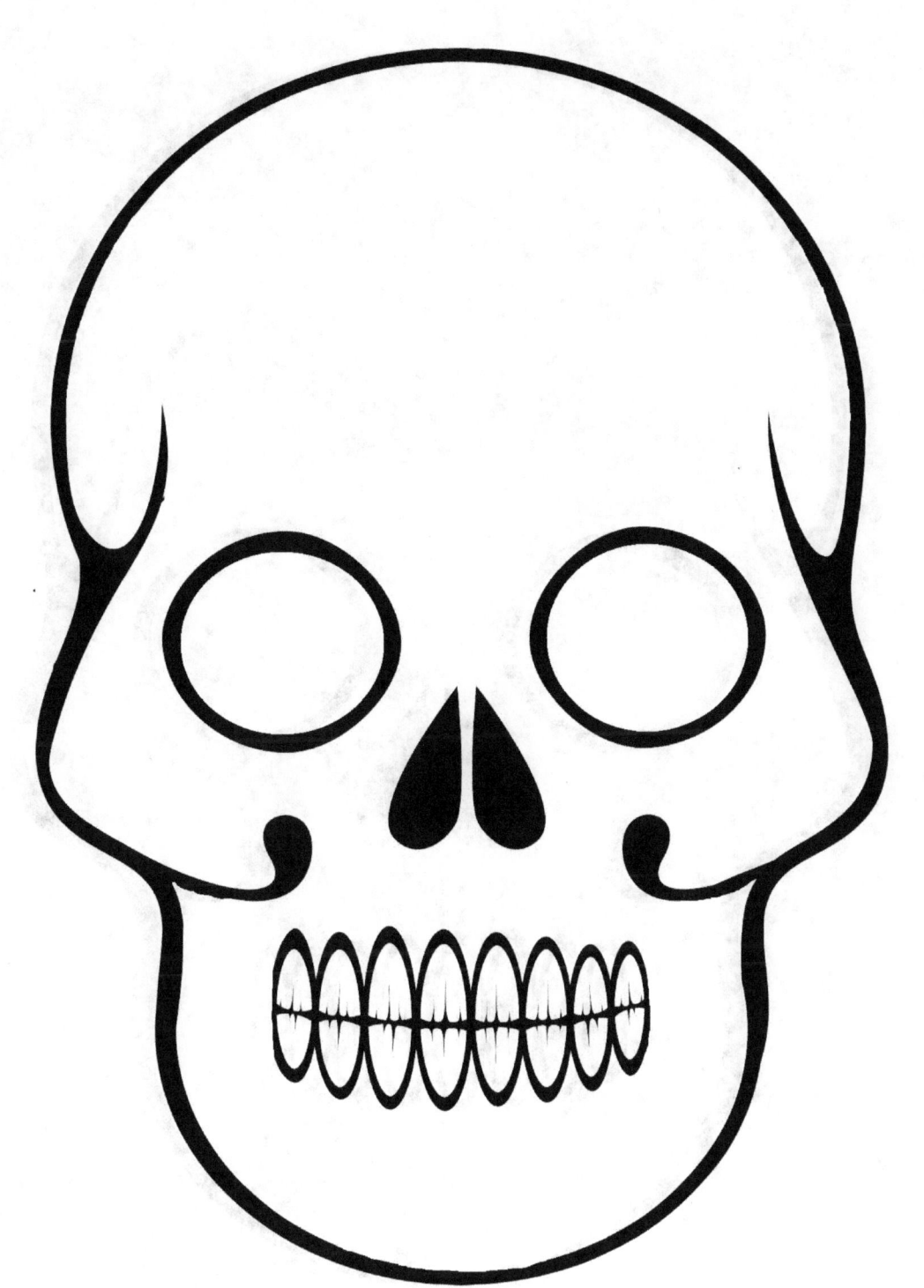

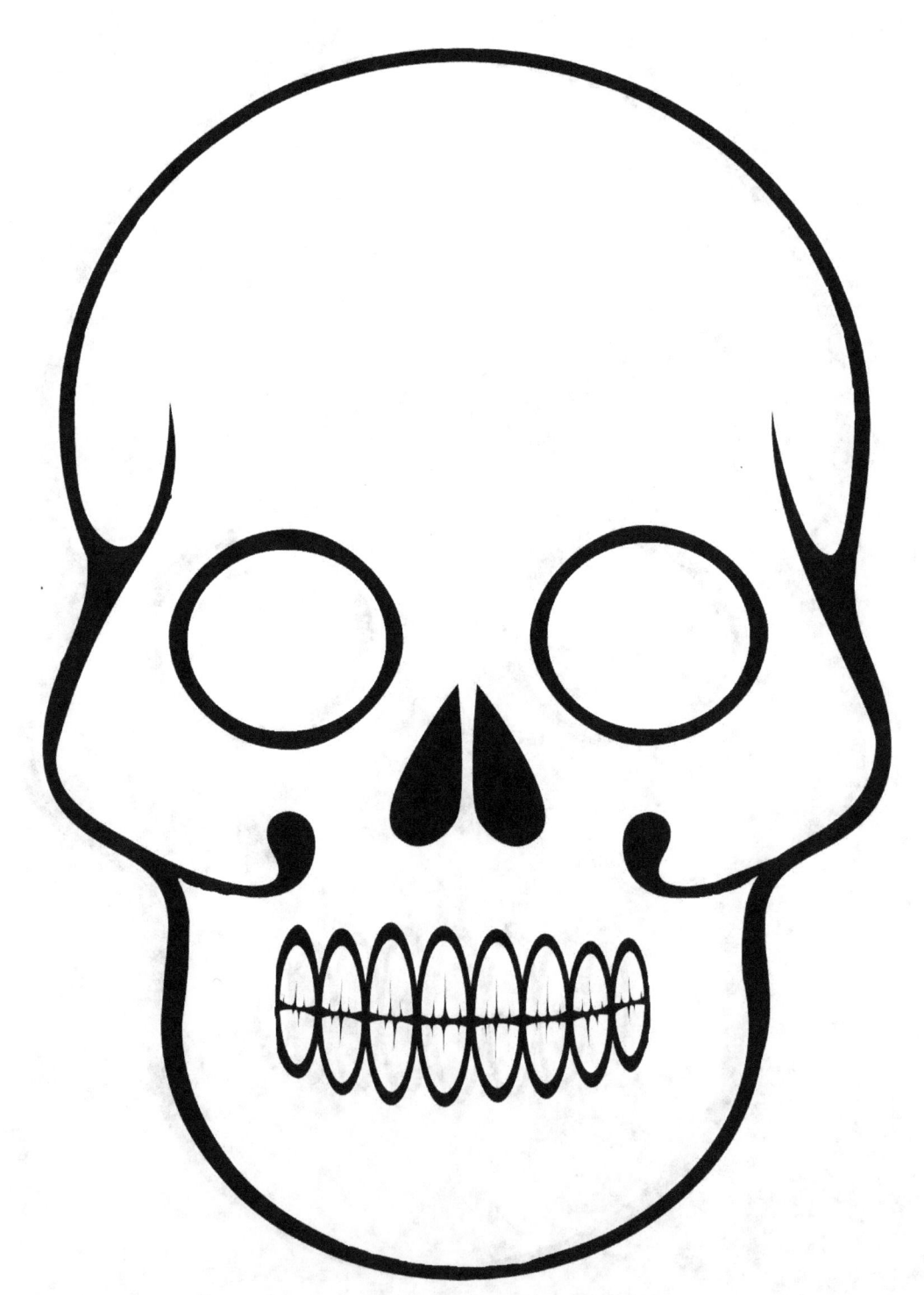

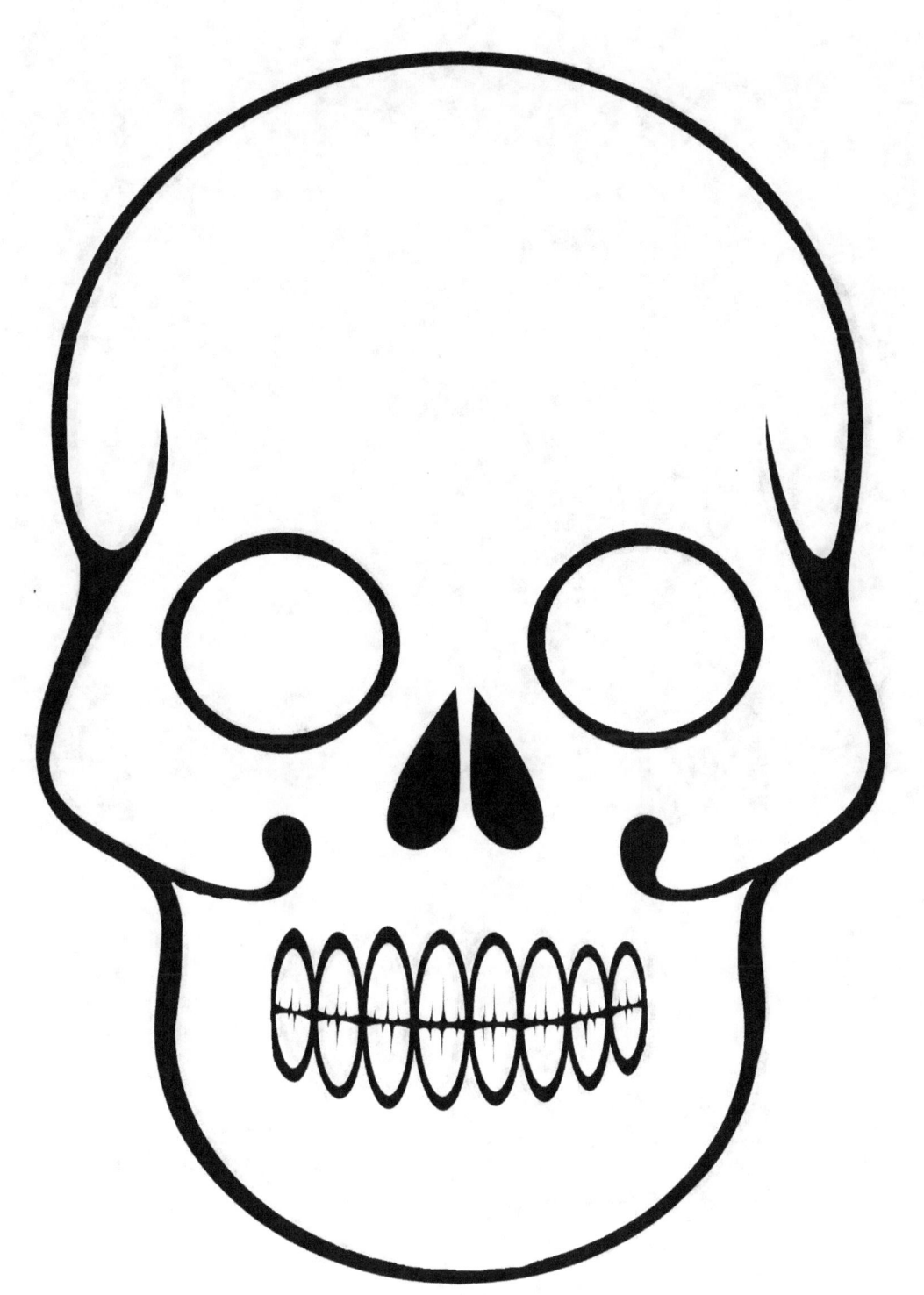

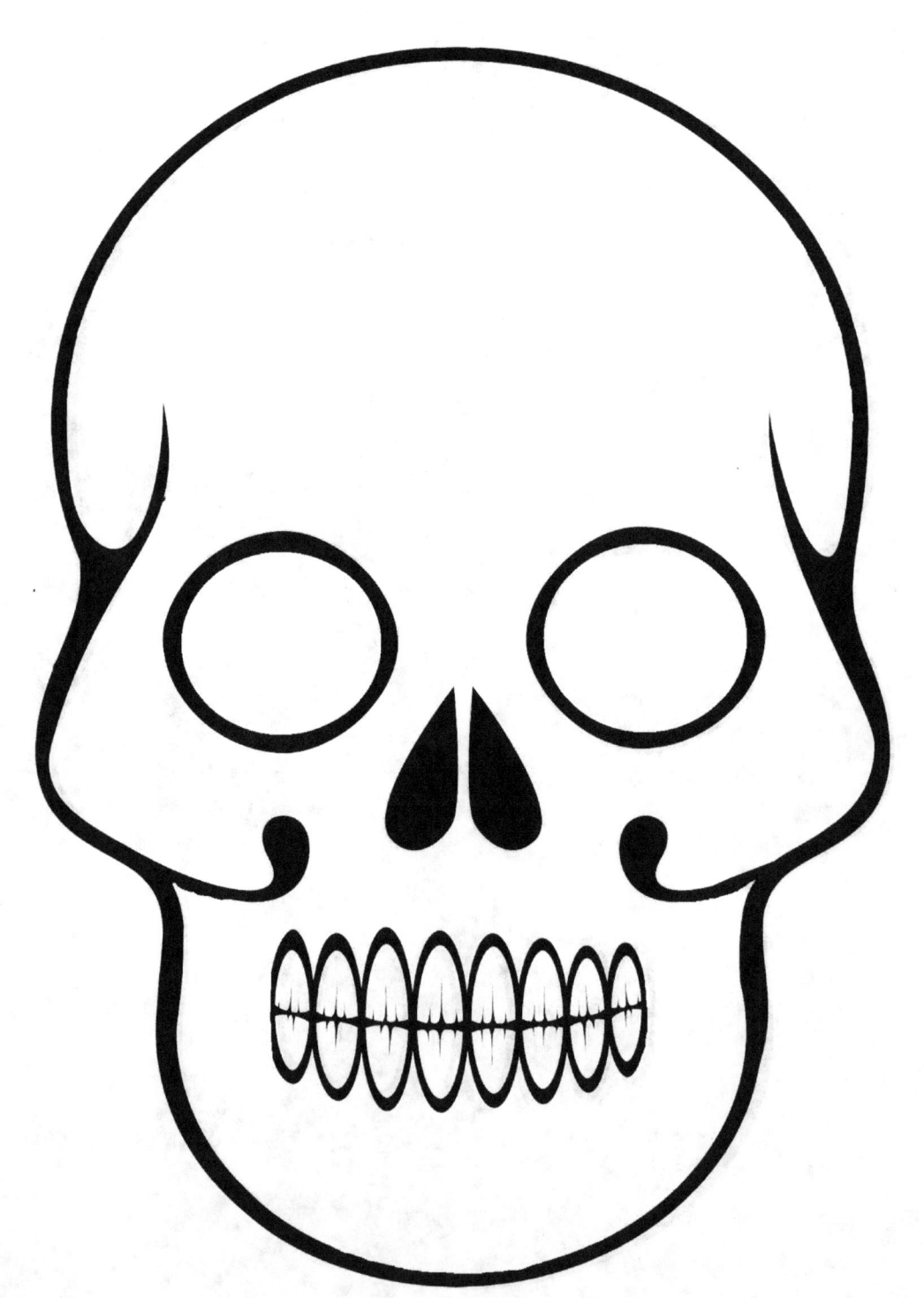

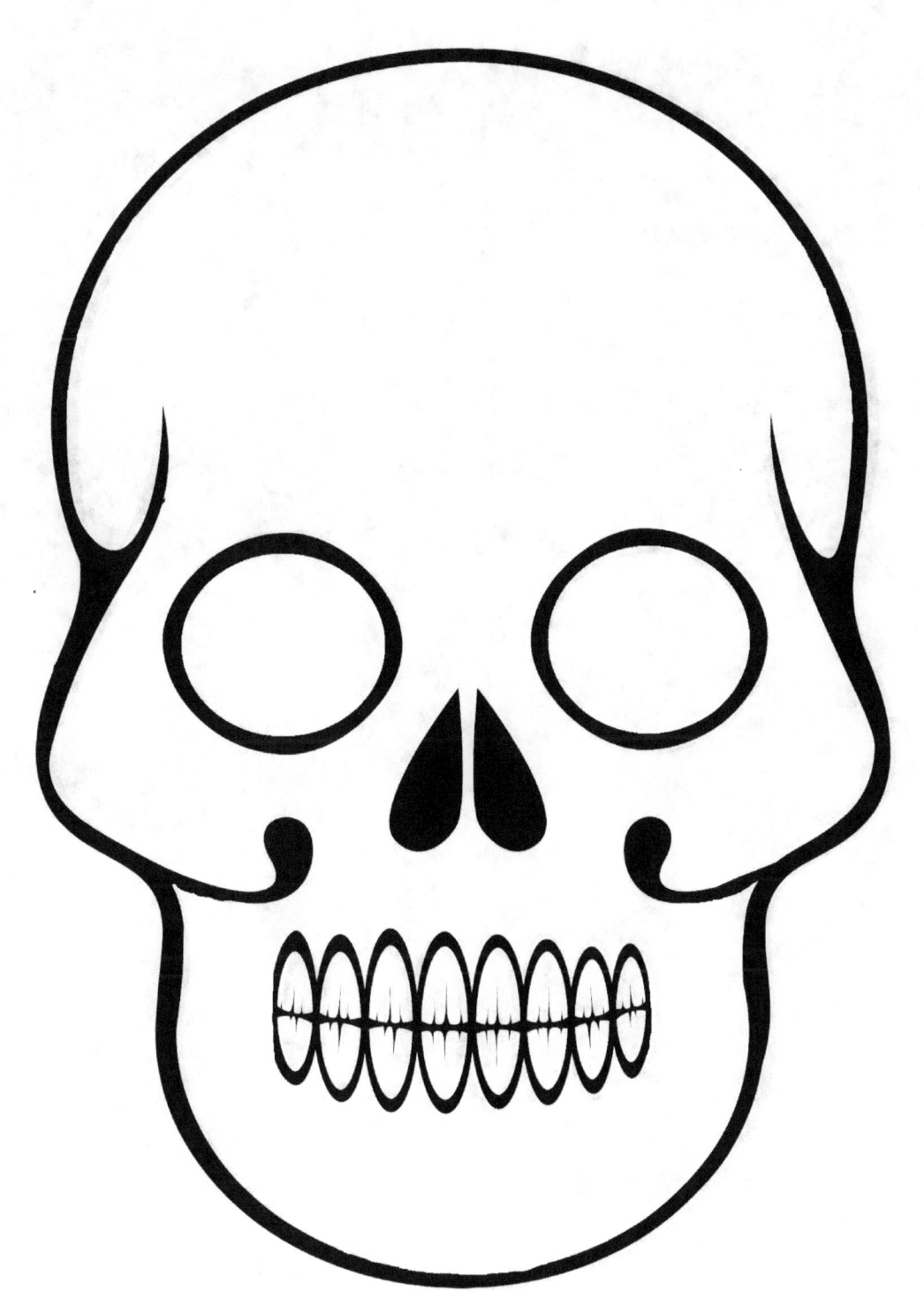

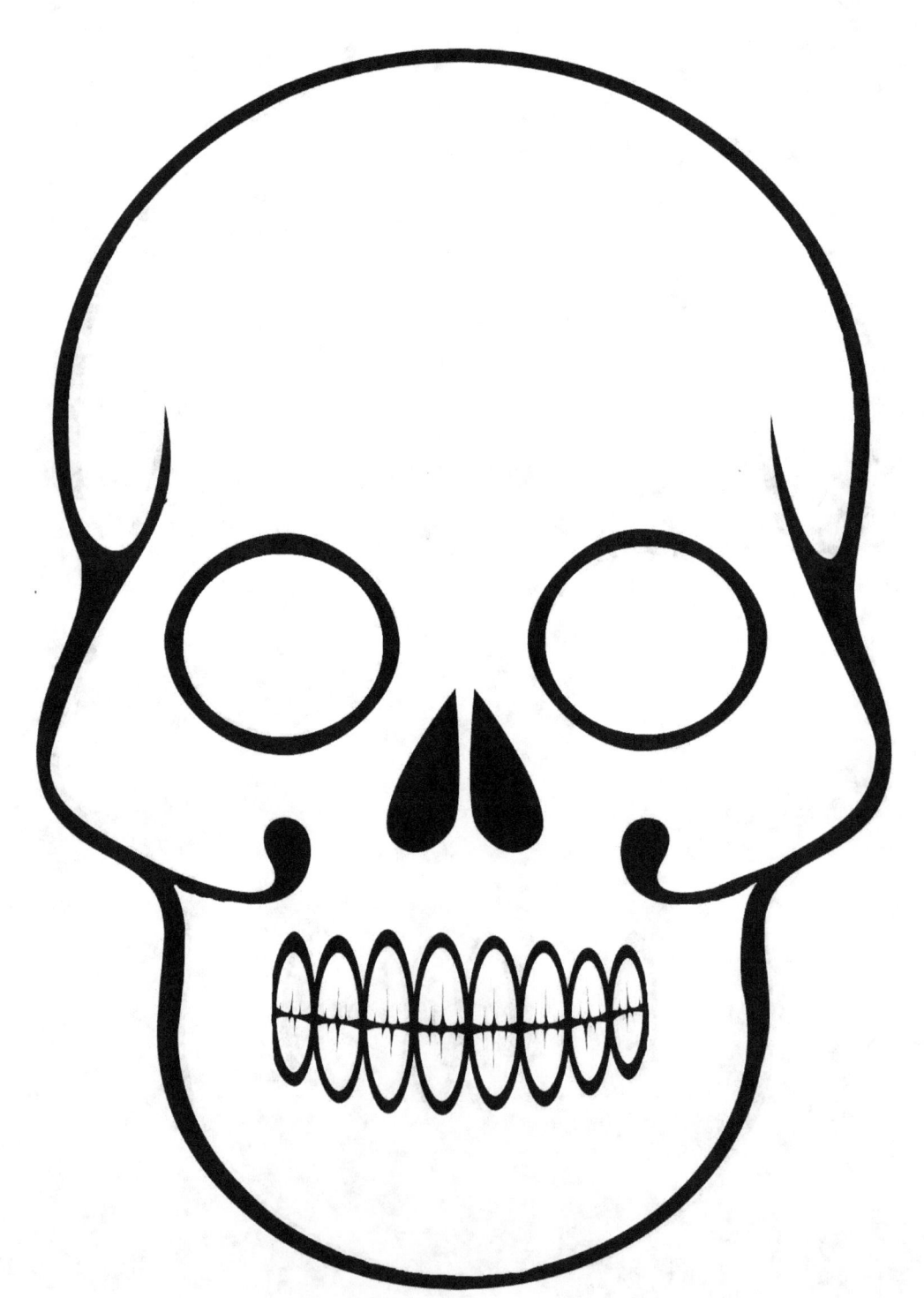

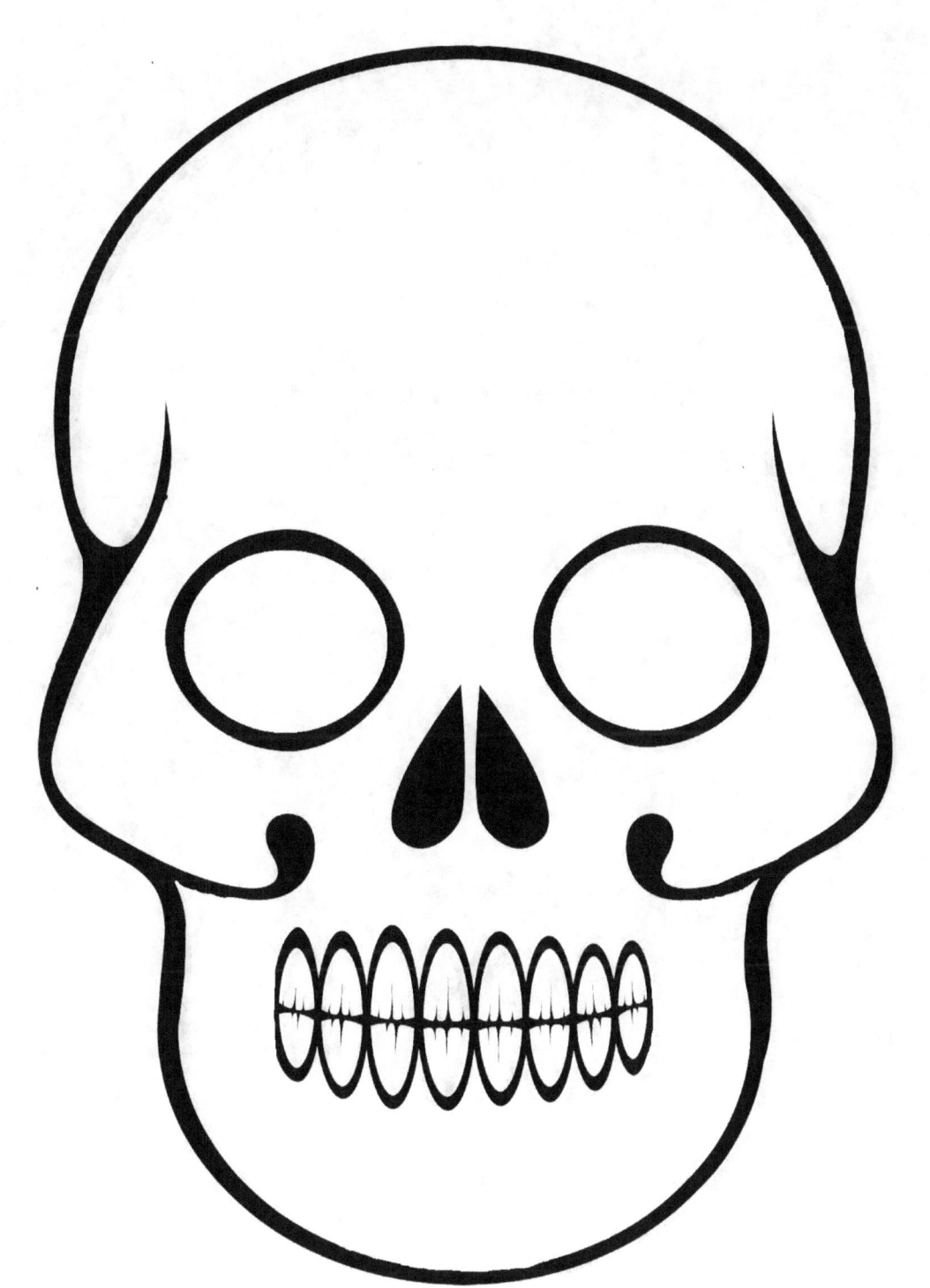

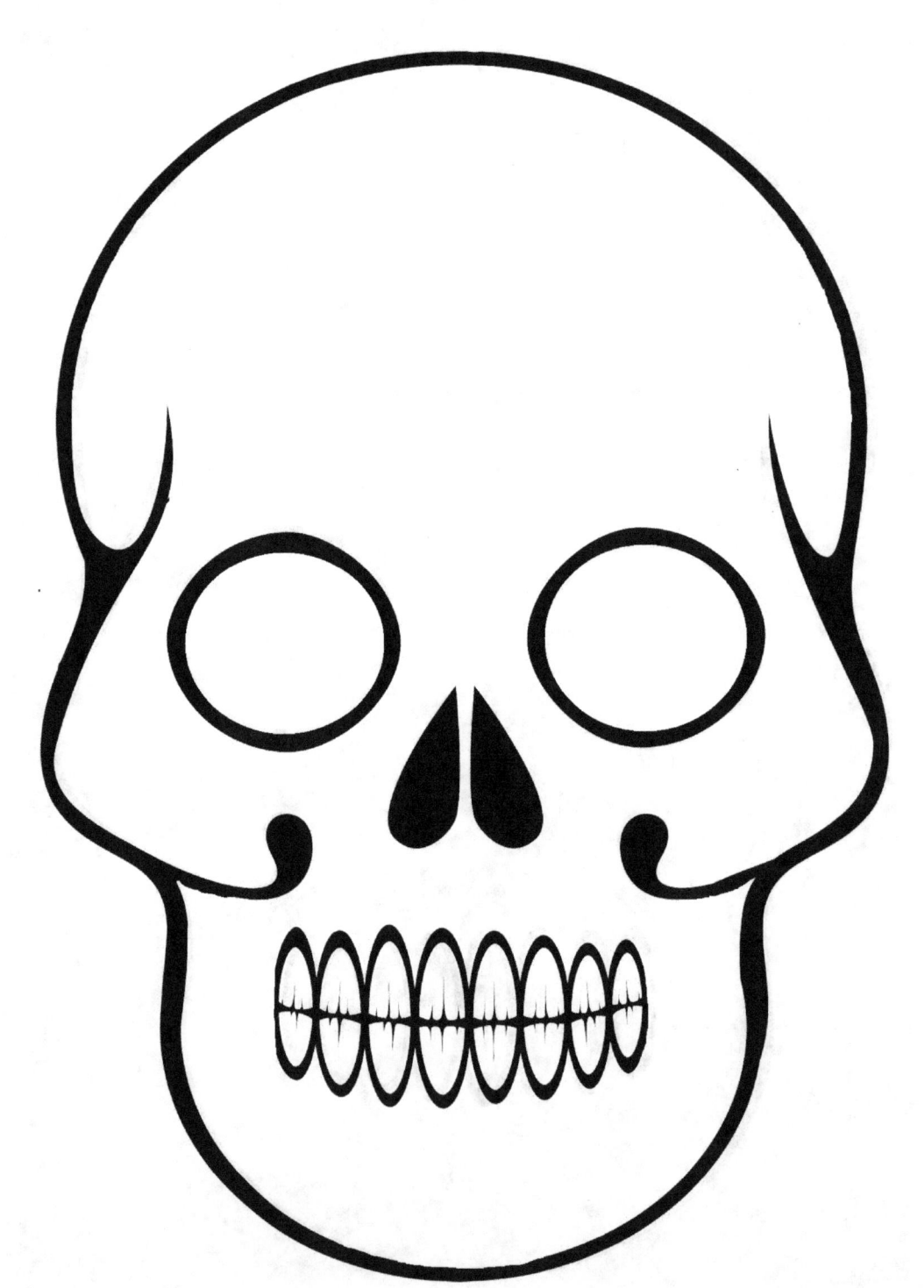

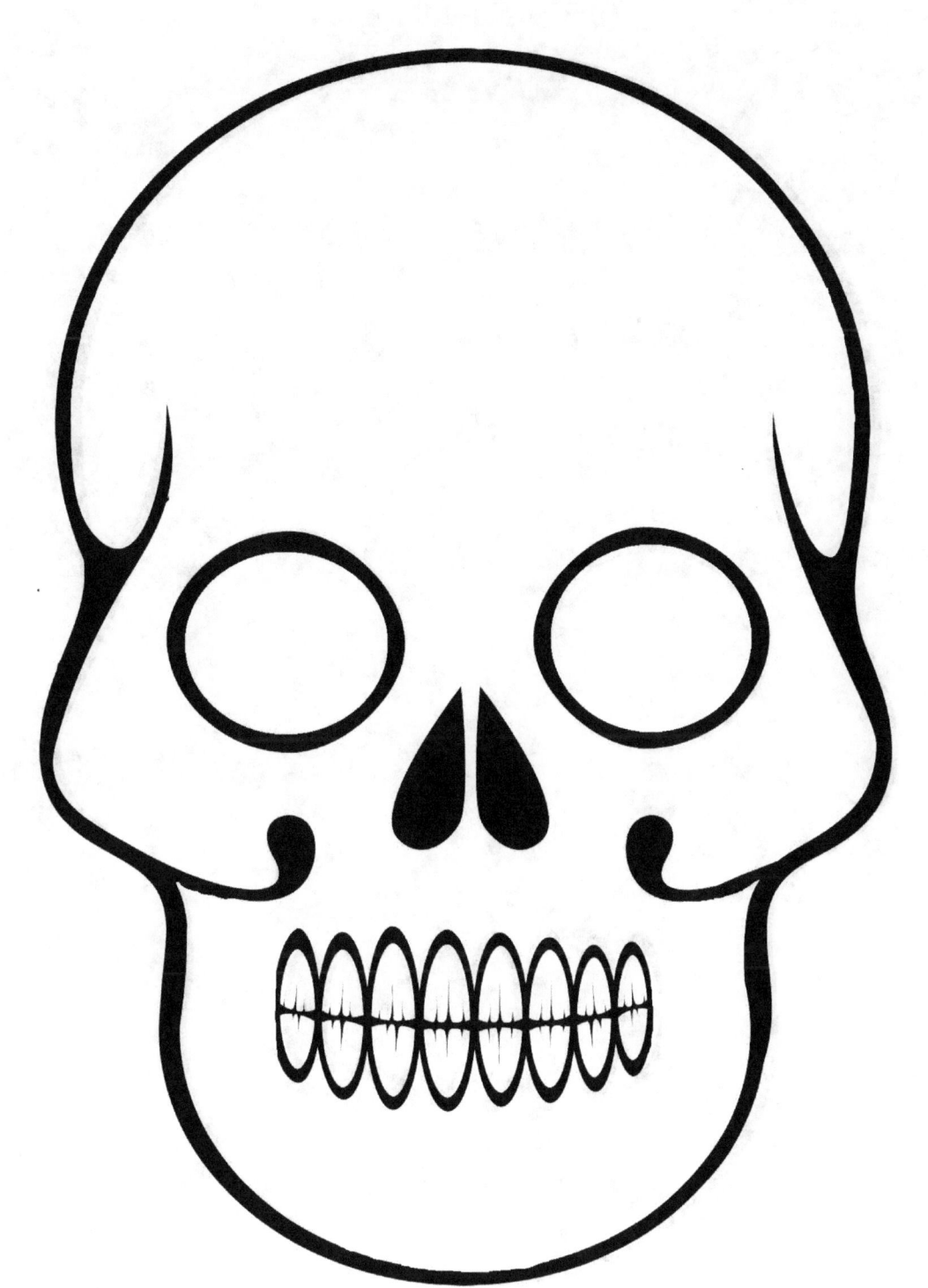

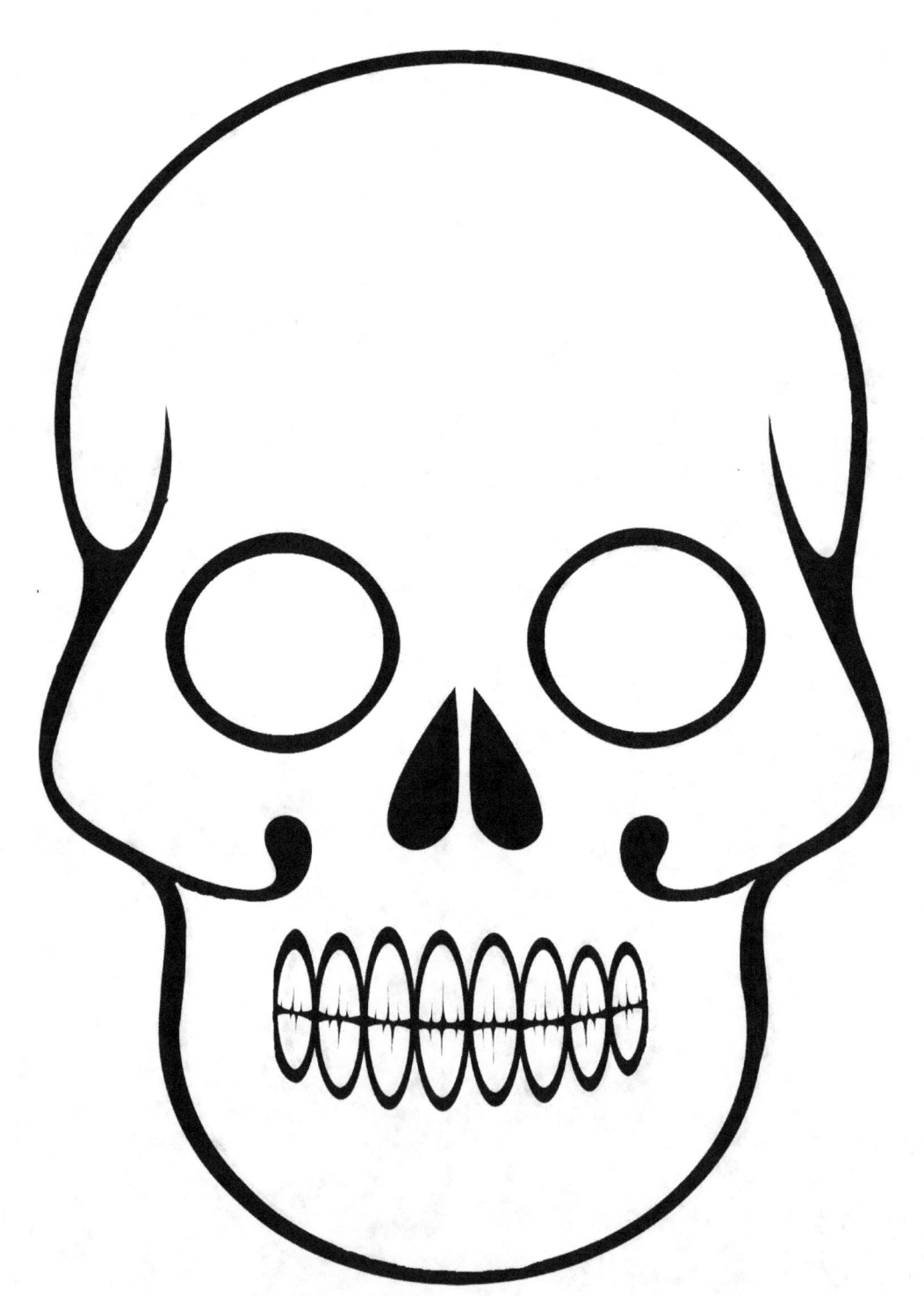

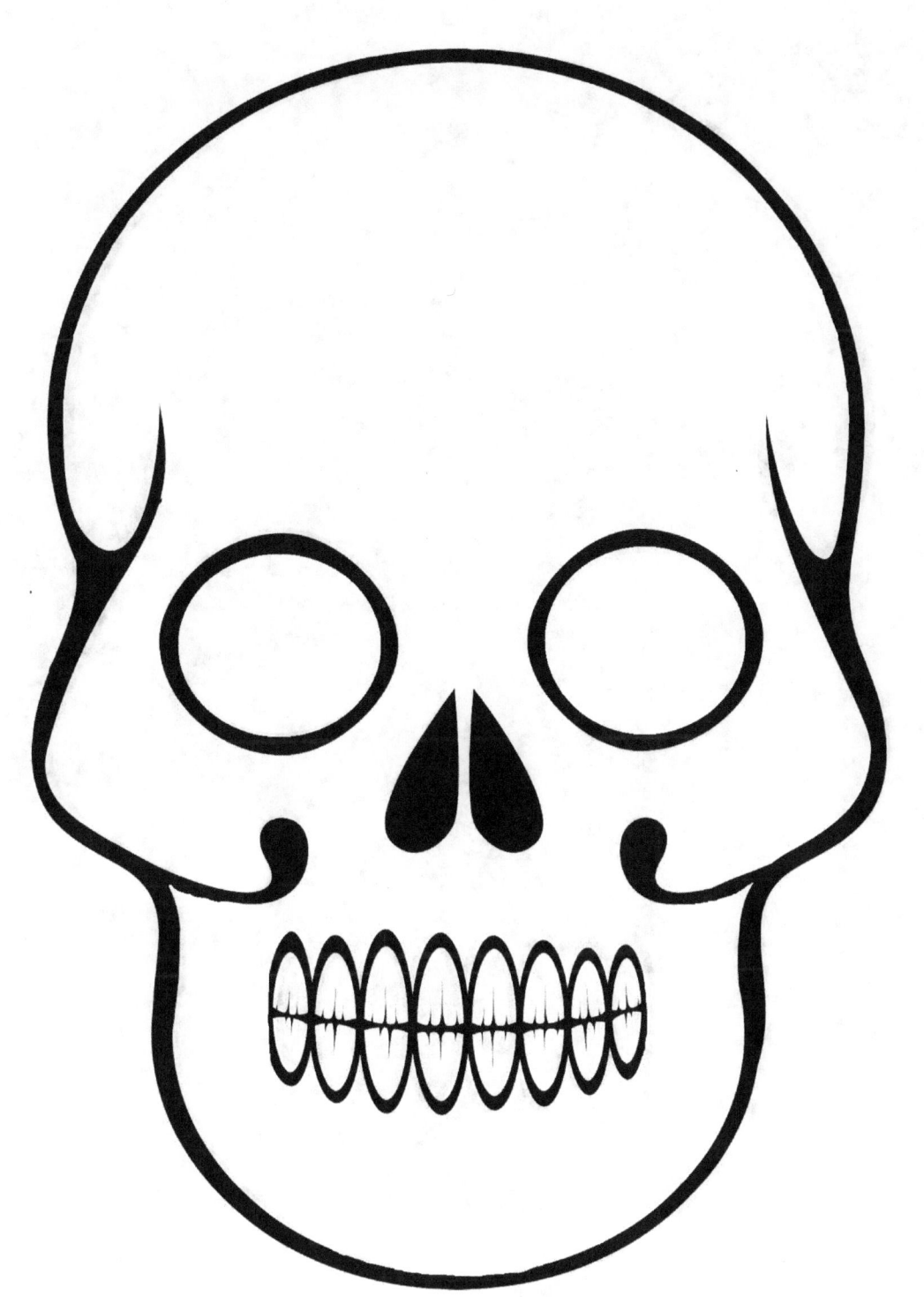

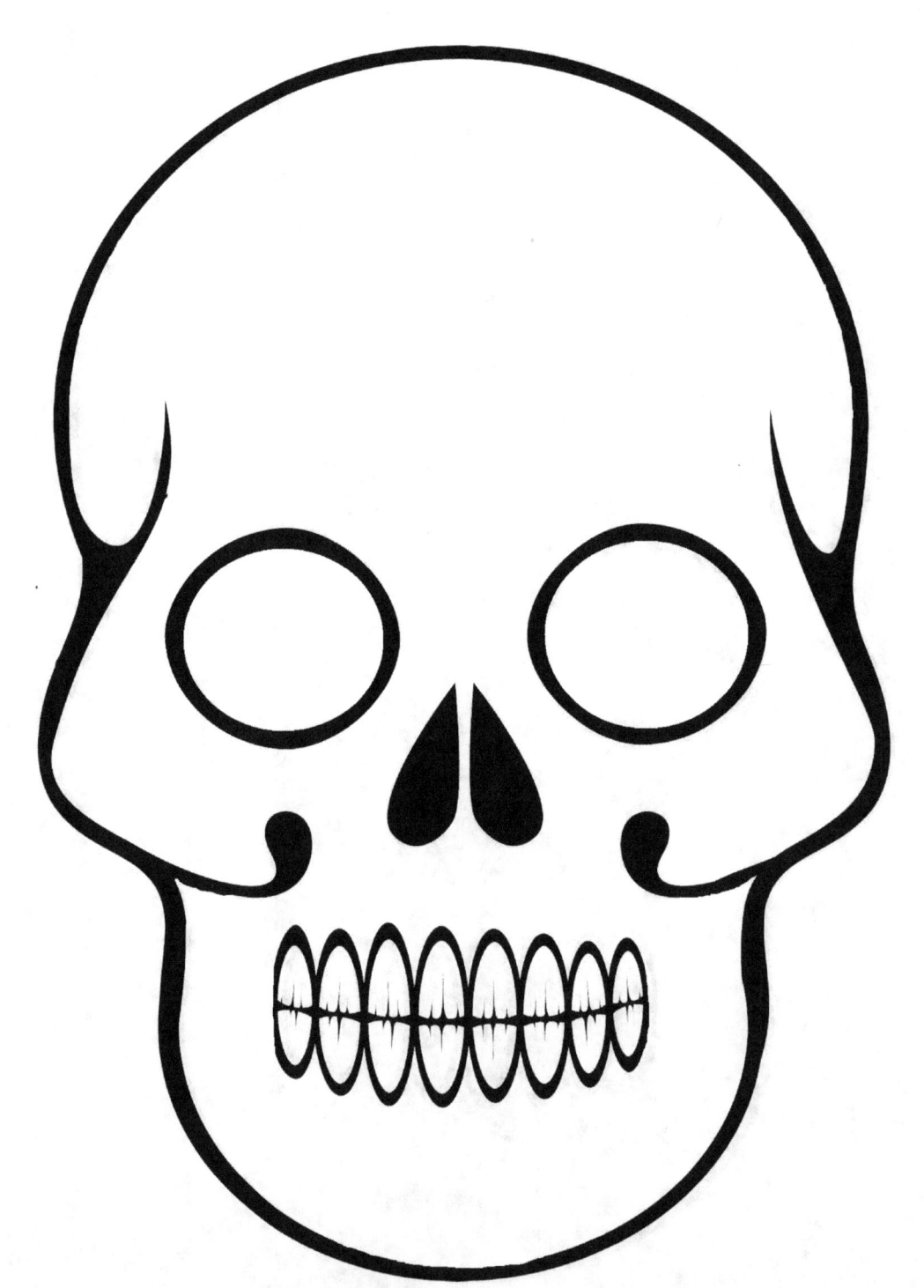

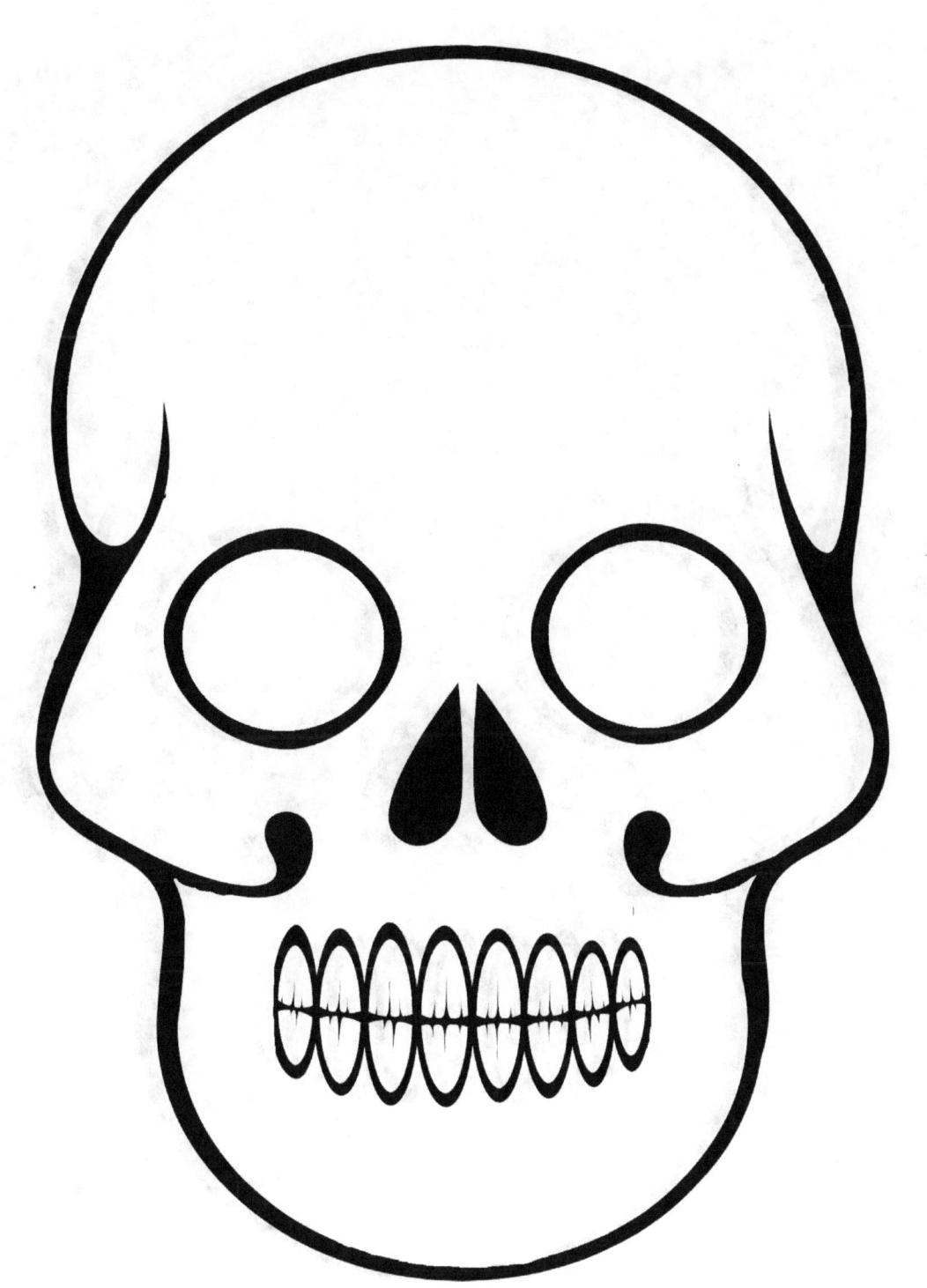

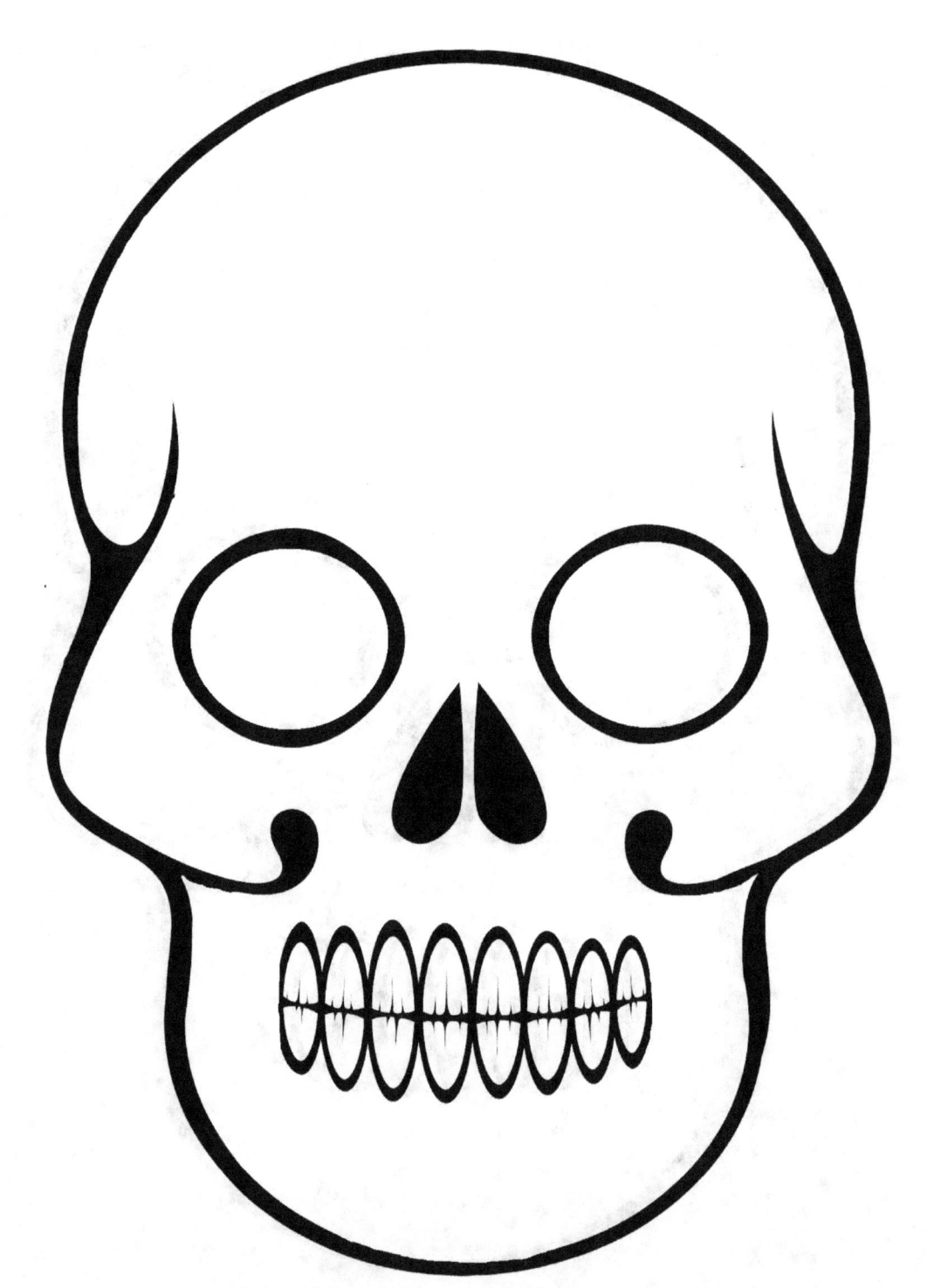

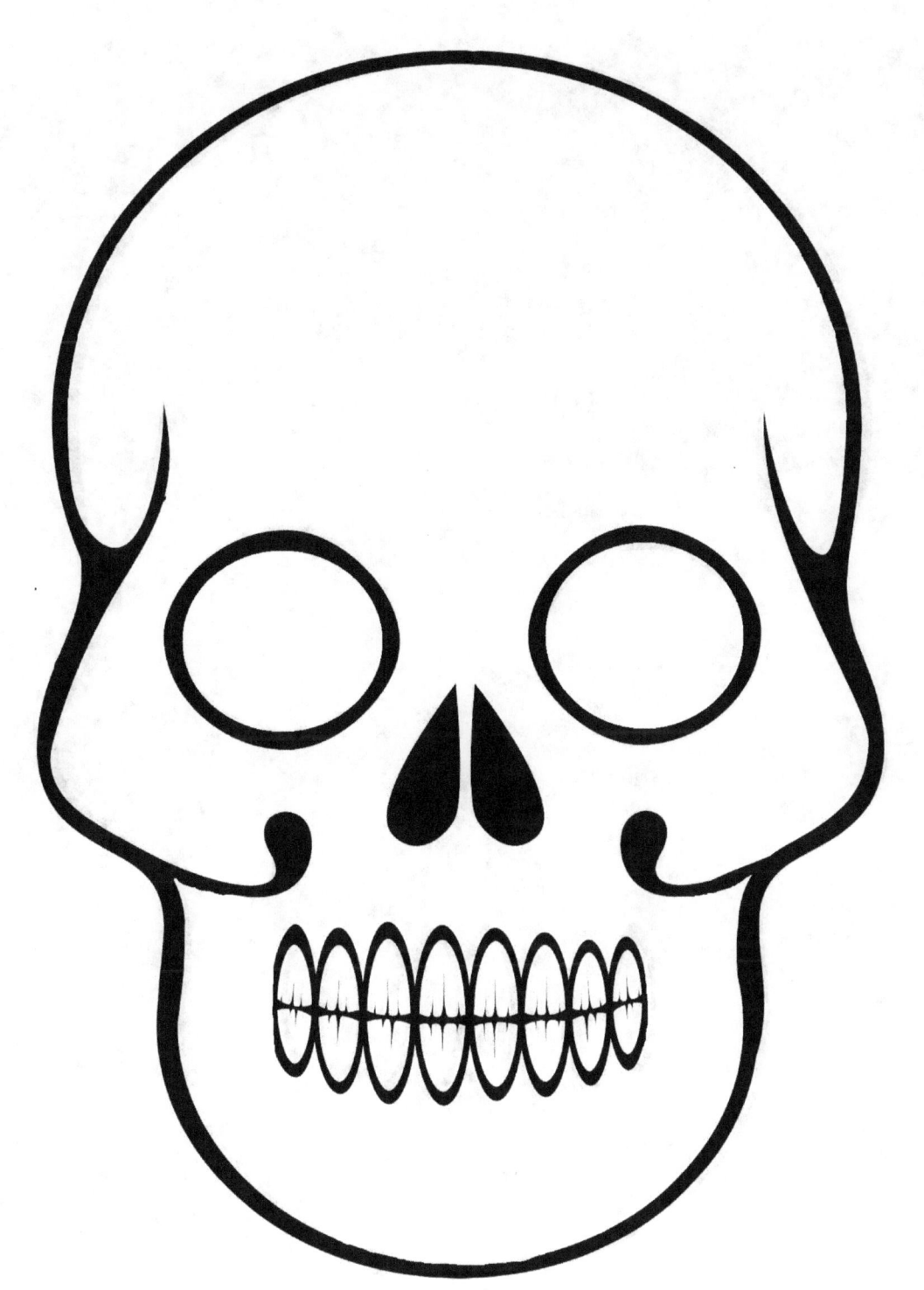

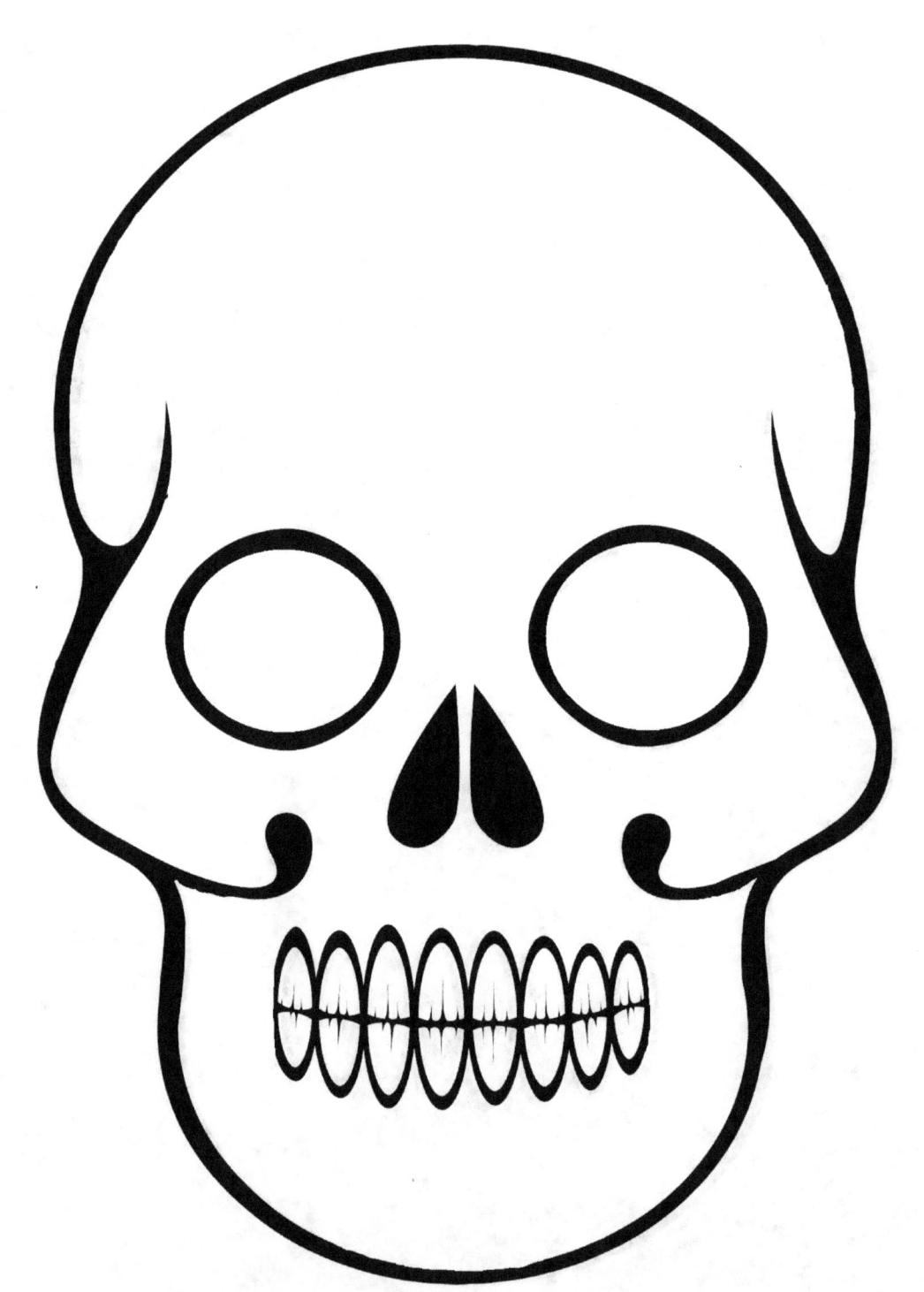

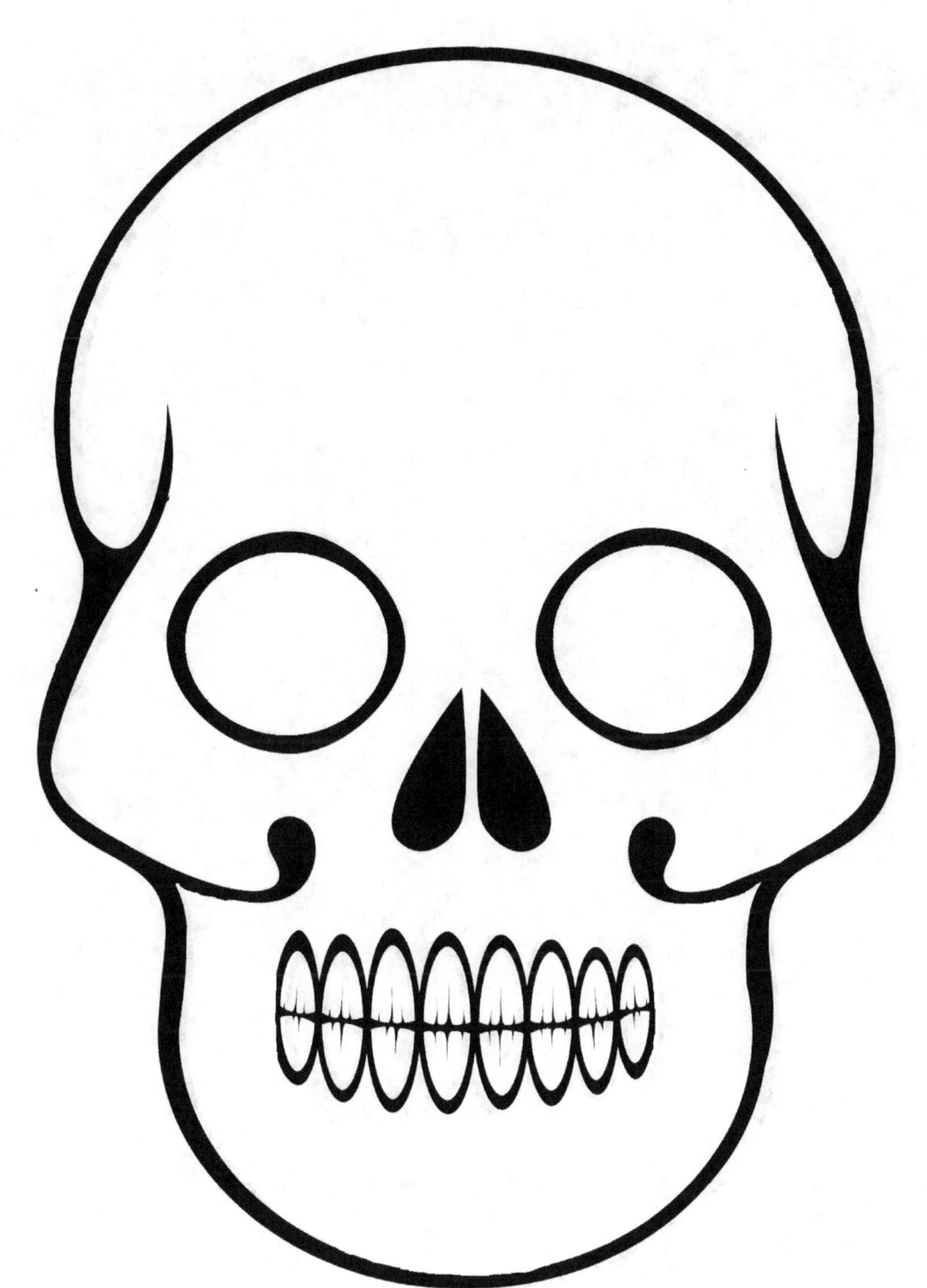

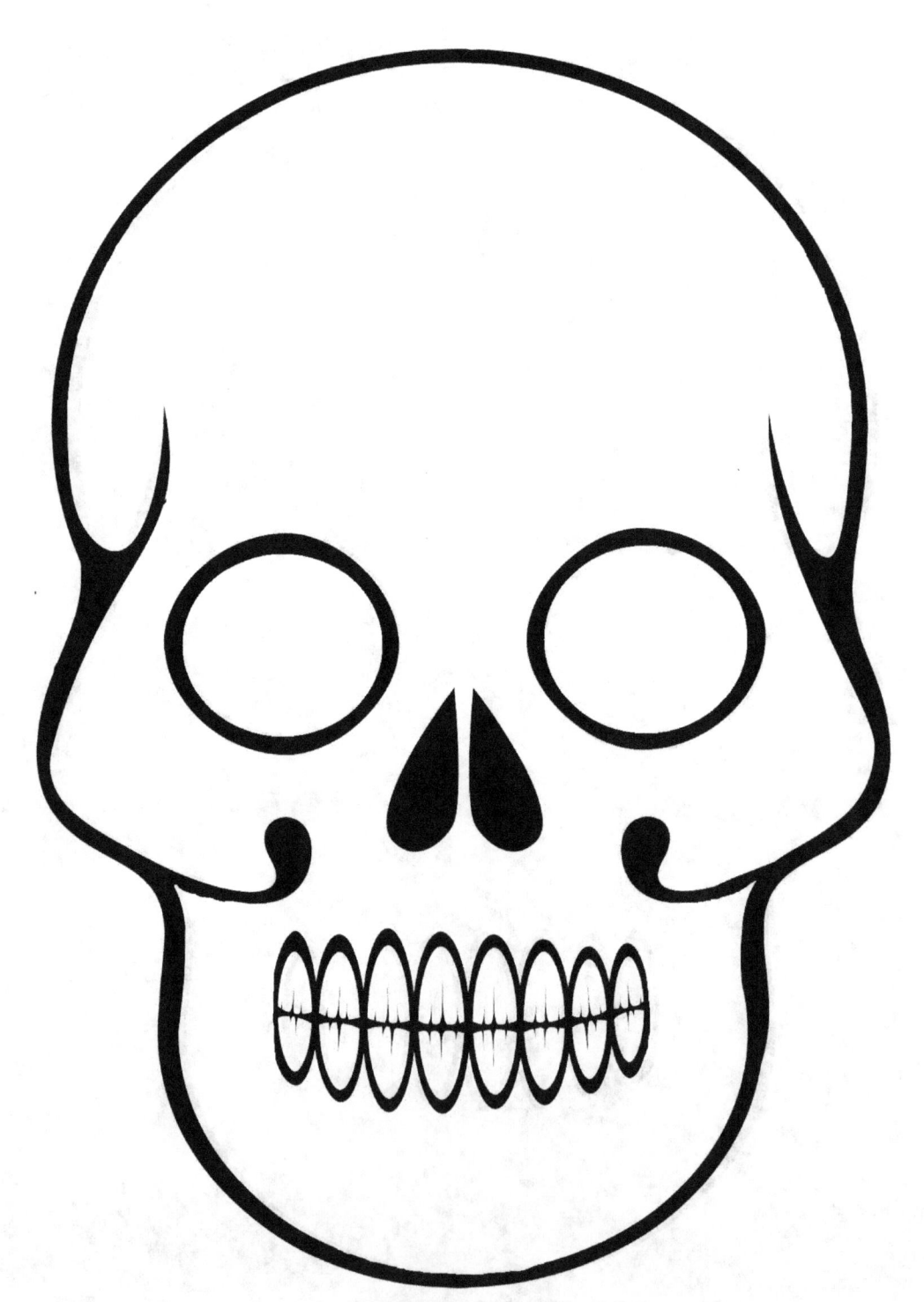

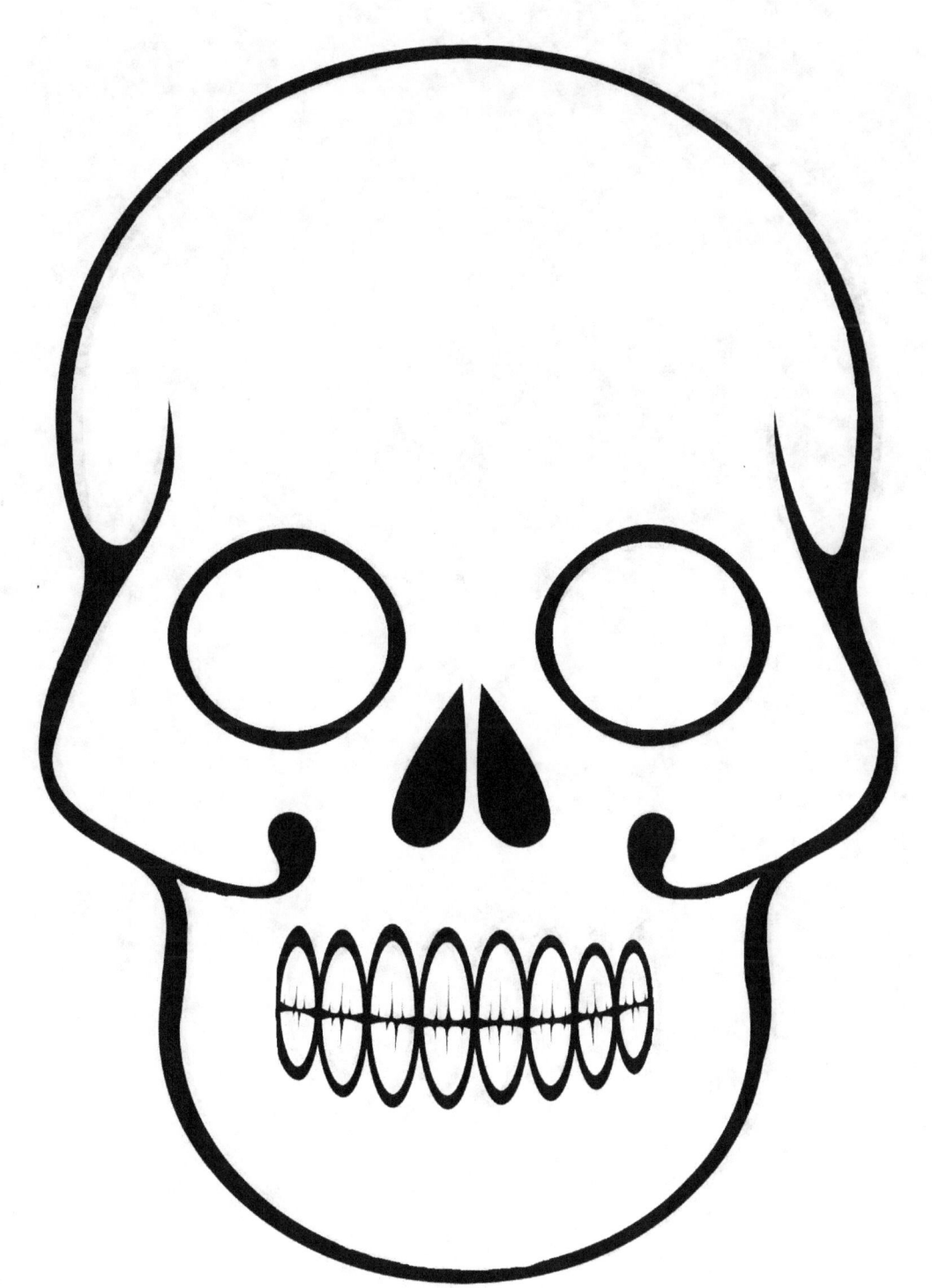

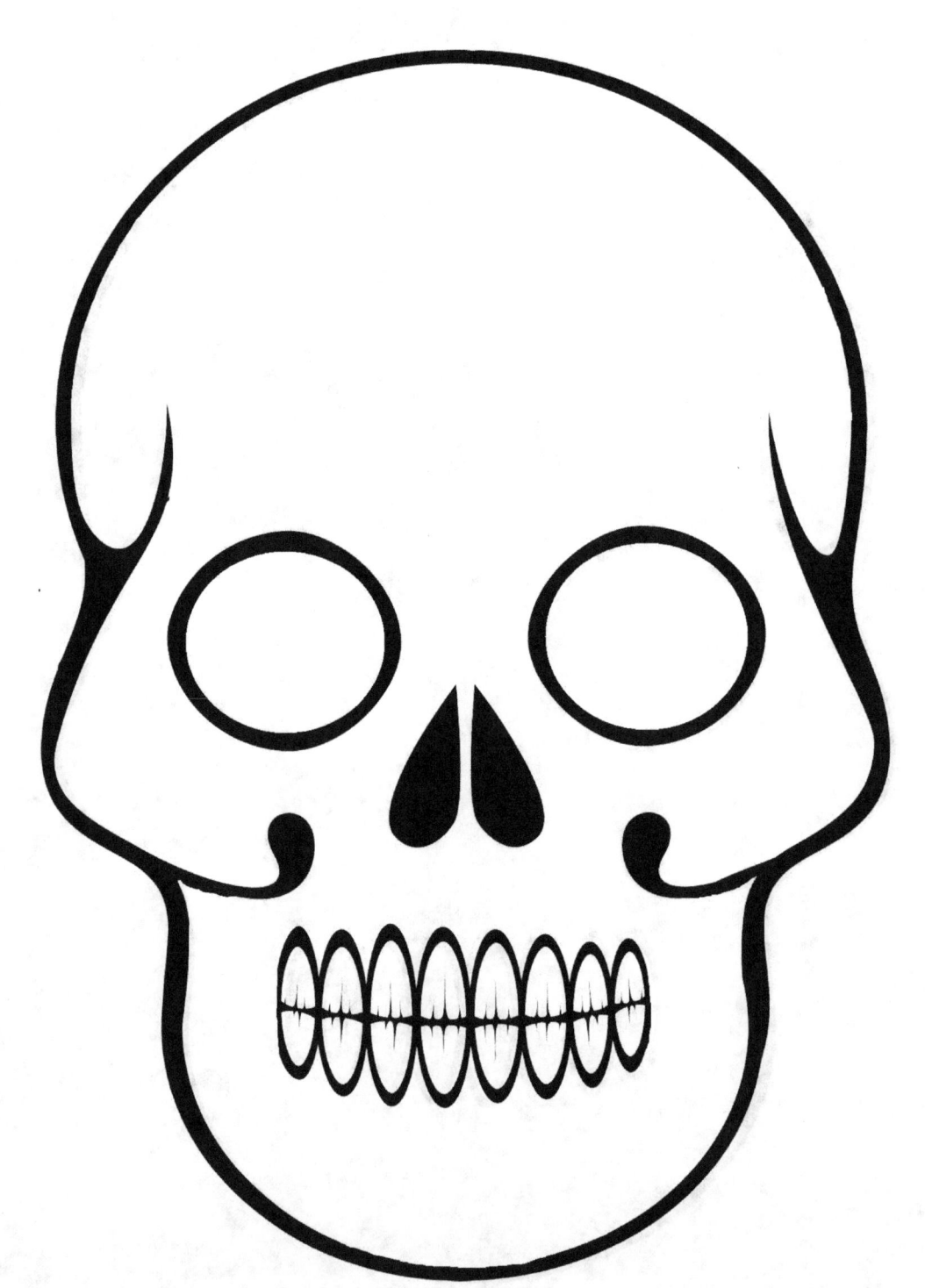

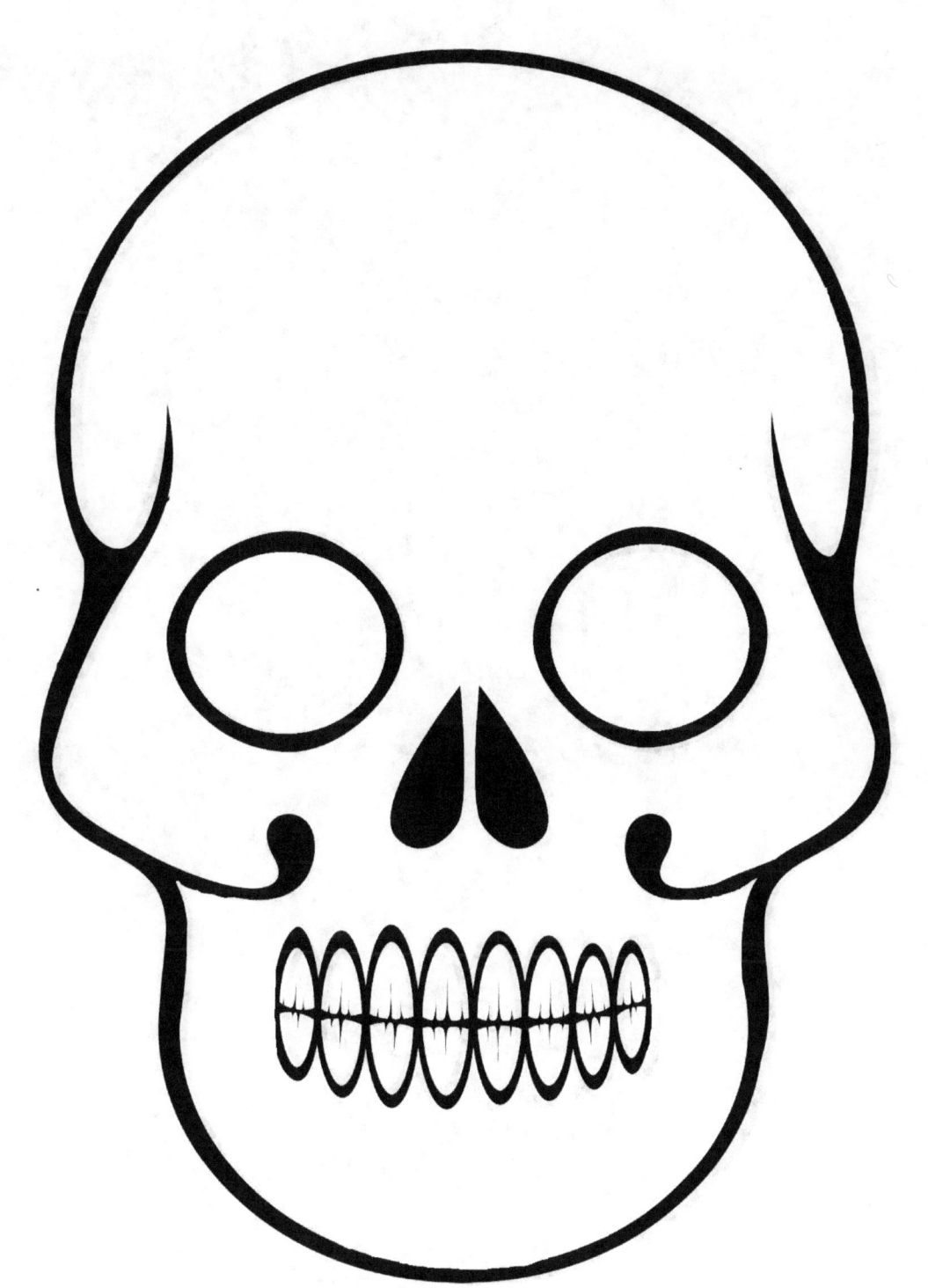

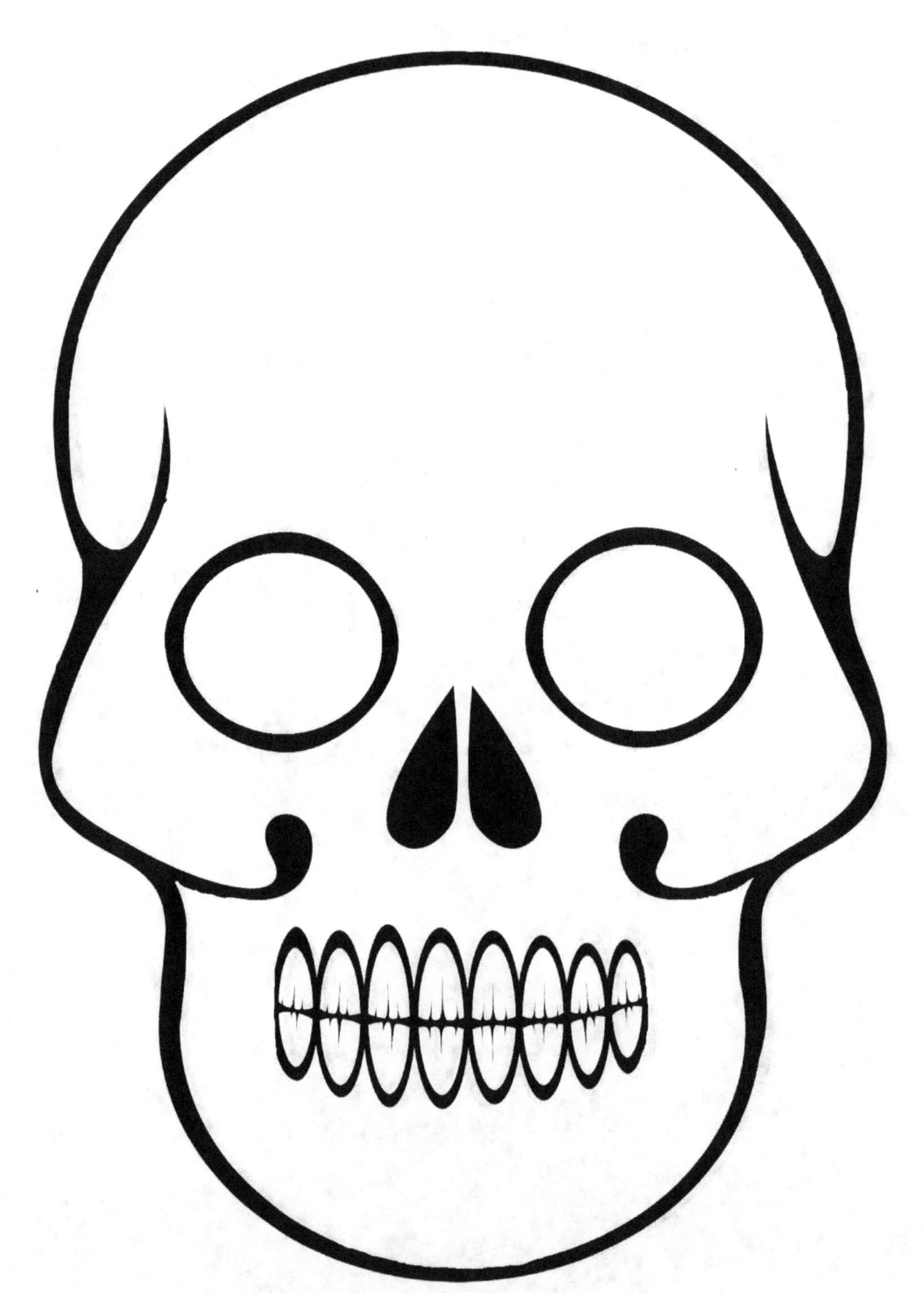

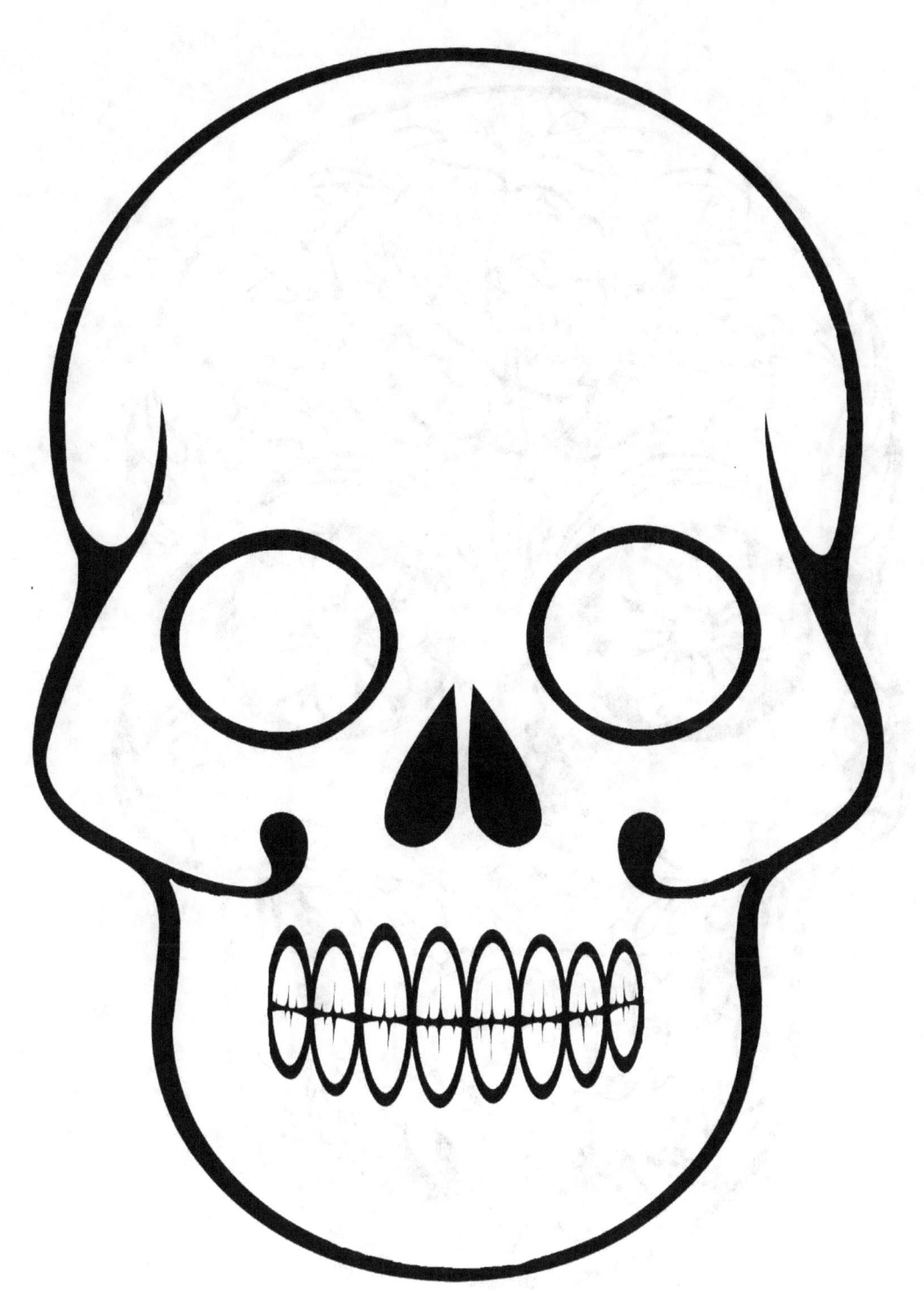

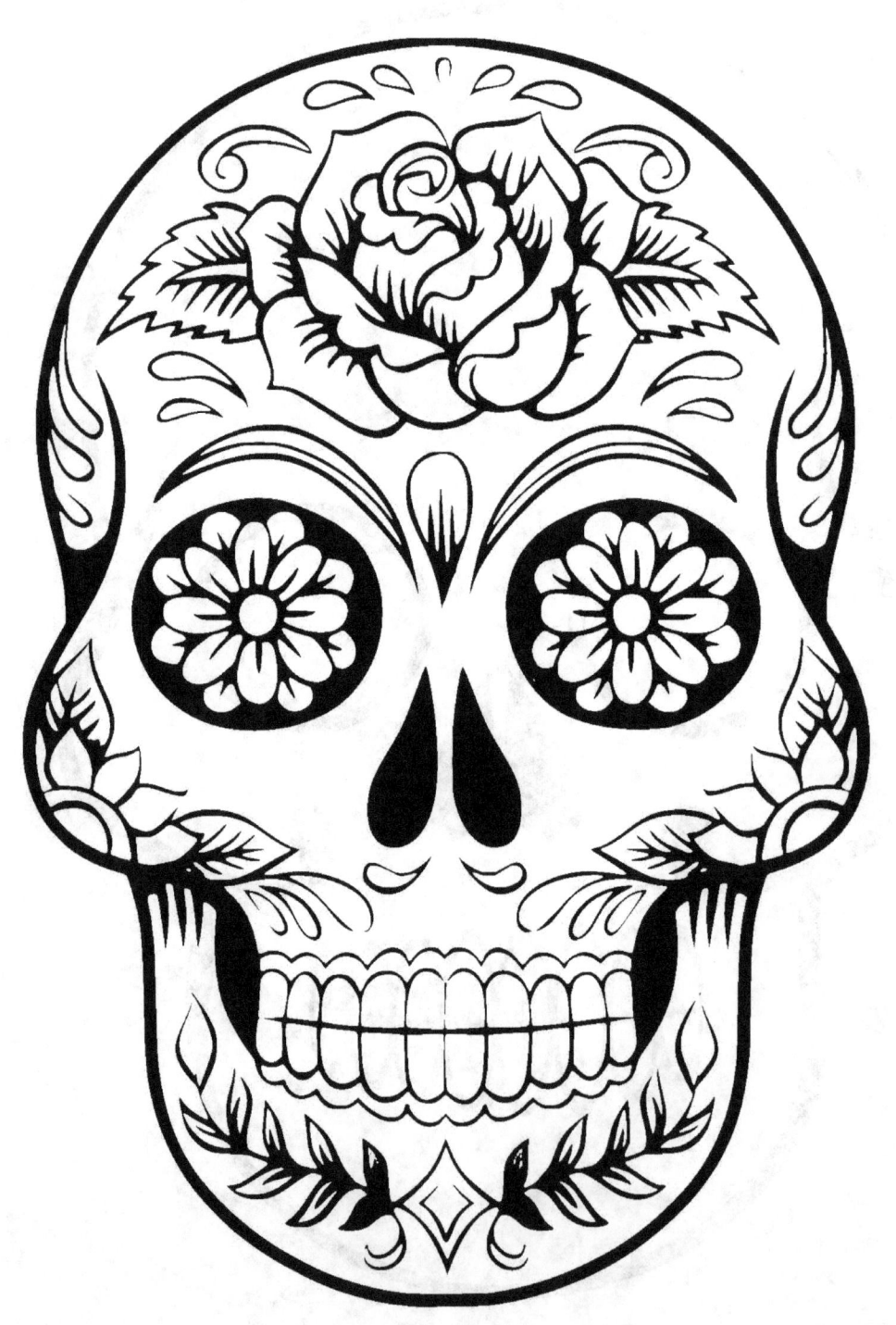

www.ingramcontent.com/pod-product-compliance
Lightning Source LLC
Chambersburg PA
CBHW081623220526
45468CB00010B/3004